NEW SCIENCE LIBRARY

presents traditional topics from a modern perspective, particularly those associated with the hard sciences—physics, biology, and medicine—and those of the human sciences—psychology, sociology, and philosophy.

The aim of this series is the enrichment of both the scientific and spiritual view of the world through their mutual dialogue and exchange.

New Science Library is an imprint of Shambhala Publications.

General editor/Ken Wilber
Consulting editors/Jeremy W. Hayward
Francisco Varela

D1508830

Also by Henry Margenau:

Ethics and Science
The Nature of Physical Reality
Open Vistas
Physics and Philosophy
Thomas and the Physics of Nineteen Fifty-Eight
Einstein's Space and Van Gogh's Sky
  (with Lawrence LeShan)
Foundations of Physics (with R. Bruce Lindsay)
Nature, Man, and Society (with Emily B. Sellon)

THE MIRACLE OF EXISTENCE

Henry Margenau

Eugene Higgins Professor Emeritus of Physics
and Natural Philosophy, Yale University

NEW SCIENCE LIBRARY
Shambhala
Boston & London
1987

New Science Library
an imprint of
Shambhala Publications, Inc.
314 Dartmouth Street
Boston, Massachusetts 02116

9 8 7 6 5 4 3 2 1

First New Science Library Edition
Original hardcover edition published by Ox Bow Press

Printed in the United States of America
Distributed in the United States by Random House
and in Canada by Random House of Canada Ltd.

Library of Congress Cataloging-in-Publication Data
Margenau, Henry, 1901–
  The miracle of existence.

  Reprint. Originally published: Woodbridge, Conn.:
Ox Bow Press, 1984.
  Bibliography: p.
  Includes index.
  1. Philosophy.   2. Science—Philosophy.
3. Religion.   I. Title.
B72.M35   1987   191   86-31526
ISBN 0-87773-407-0 (pbk.)

Dedicated to my dear wife Liesel and my children Rolf, Annemarie and Henry, Jr.

Contents

Preface

The title of this book was intended to characterize its philosophic content, which couples a theory of knowledge with compatible and embracive metaphysical conclusions. These ideas turn out to be akin to certain widely accepted and remarkably enduring oriental views. Hence the title "The Meeting of East and West" would also have been appropriate. But it was preempted by the famous book of that name (reprinted 1979, Ox Bow Press) published by my old teacher and friend, Filmer S. C. Northrop, to whom I wish to express my gratitude for having led my thoughts in these directions.

Choice of topics and the writing of the text were greatly influenced and aided by discussions with Harold Morowitz, the distinguished Professor of Biophysics and Biochemistry and a cordial friend. To him I wish to express my most sincere thanks.

THE MIRACLE
OF EXISTENCE

Introduction

This book attempts a synthesis of science, philosophy, and religion. It is a sequel to two earlier books[1,2] in which some of the issues here presented are treated in more conventional ways. The present volume, conceived and written during the late years of my life, departs from convention, at least with respect to western thought, and takes risks I would have forgone in my earlier writings.

The philosophy underlying it is a form of idealism, of which a few words might be said. Idealism stands in contrast to realism, a view that takes things to be in essence as they appear and makes the best of them. The realist, however, is easily embarrassed by the question "Why is there anything at all?" He either shrugs this off or turns at once to a religion, and usually one at odds with science. *Or as a 'nonsense' question*

Idealism is well defined by J. H. Muirhead in the *Encyclopedia Britannica* (1944 edition):

epistemological
def.

> Idealism as a philosophical doctrine conceives of knowledge or [= ? *sense of* 'or'?] experience as a process in which the two factors of subject and object stand in a relation of (entire) [*not partial*] interdependence on each other as warp and woof. Apart from the activity of the self as *[is this implying an ontological idealism? No separation of idealism phenomena + noumena?]* subject in sensory reaction, memory and association, imagination, judgment and inference there can be no world of objects. A thing in itself which is not a thing to some consciousness is an entirely unrealizable, because contradictory, conception.

To characterize the doctrine in terms of examples I review very briefly the contributions of three idealist philosophers of the early modern era. The first, who had a strong influence on the other two, is Leibnitz. He is critical of the view of Des-

M's def. of 'realism': 'a view that takes things to be in essence as they appear and makes the best of them' Hence, an epistemological realism is what he has in mind what does M. mean by "makes the best of them"?

Force as power to persist in being as prime. √∃x.

cartes, the proponent of a dualism between matter, which he
calls *res extensa,* and mind, his *res cogitans.* Leibnitz asks: "Is
matter nothing but *res extensa,* mind nothing but *res cogitans?*"
"Have these *res* no other attributes?" His answer is that matter
has inertia, mind has the "power" of persisting through states
and degrees of consciousness. This attribute of persistence,
present in both matter and mind, Leibnitz calls a "force," using
this term in a sense wholly different from the one now adopted,
which was introduced by Newton, a contemporary of Leibnitz's." He then takes force, this "power" of persistence, to be
the reality, the metaphysical principle of existence.

These steps may be difficult to follow, especially because of
the antiquated use of terms. But the conclusions drawn from
them characterize one of the first modern idealistic systems of
the West. For Leibnitz's reasoning goes on: Force is not one; it
is many. No two objects can occupy the same space, no two
minds or consciousnesses can flow together. There is an infinity
of forces. Each is unextended (because it is the property of
reality *besides* extension); hence it is indivisible, simple. He
calls it a monad, or center of force, a term he took over from
Giordano Bruno, the Italian philosopher who lived a century
earlier.

i.e., principle of identity?

The next questions Leibnitz asks are "How can there be
many monads if each is unextended?" "What distinguishes
them?" His answer assumes the thesis of the "identity of
indiscernibles." But monads are different in the degree of
self-representation, hence they are not alike. All of them,
including those of matter, have some degree of consciousness.

extension (or matter) as principle of individuation now self-representation

What, then, is the external world; why are its objects extended? Because extension is the manner in which a monad
represents to itself its own exclusion from other monads. Leibnitz's complete answer, however, involves God, the most per-
fect monad, that is, the monad of highest degree of self-representation. Every monad reflects, more or less imperfectly, the
contents of the divine mind. The principle of the identity of
indiscernibles has occasionally been used to claim the sameness,

macro/ micro ανάλογη

the oneness, of all minds. A slightly different interpretation is given by Leibnitz's simile, which relates to different minds being exposed to the same external situation and judging it to be the same. Leibnitz likens men to prisoners in isolated cells, and the warden (the supreme monad) projects a story of his own choosing on screens of different sizes in different cells. The modern reader will find Leibnitz's reasoning difficult to accept; nevertheless its high flight from sensory experience to God is impressive and his effect on later philosophers, especially the two I am about to mention, was strong.

George Berkeley, the Irish bishop, is my next choice. In brief, Berkeley denies the existence of what previous philosophers called "primary qualities," the basic qualities exhibited by matter, such as distance between things, magnitude, and situation. As to the latter, he uses the argument that the eye sees things upside down, denying the fact that body 1 can be said to be above body 2. And if there are no primary qualities, or if their nature is elusive, the whole external world is an illusion.

Continuing this kind of reasoning Berkeley concludes that external things are produced by the will of the divine intelligence. They are caused—and caused in a regular order. To quote from the brief but pointed description of Berkeley's philosophy in the *British Encyclopedia* (R. Adamson):

> There exist in the divine mind archetypes, of which sense experience may be said to be the realization in our finite minds. Our belief in the permanence of something which corresponds to the association in our mind of actual and possible sensations means belief in the orderliness of nature, and that is merely assurance that the universe is regulated by mind. . . . Physical science, in trying to interpret the divine language of which natural things are the words and letters, merely strives to bring human conceptions into harmony with the divine thoughts.

The implication that mind creates the objects it sees evidently created some misunderstanding among students at Oxford University, where Berkeley ended his career. The following limerick explains it and ends our discussion of this highly competent and literate philosopher.

> There was a young man who said "God,
> to you it must seem very odd
>   that a tree as a tree
>   simply ceases to be
> when there's no one about in the quad."

God answers:

> "Young man, your astonishment's odd,
> I'm always about in the quad
>   and that's why the tree
>   never ceases to be
> as observed by, yours faithfully, God."

Leibnitz and Berkeley, along with other philosophers of this era, took few steps from the science they knew into religion, ignoring a large part of the landscape. Had they known modern science, they would doubtless have added arguments like the following to their discourse. A fact so peculiar yet commonplace that it fails to amaze the modern scientist is the sameness of the properties of the elementary constituents of matter. Every grade school pupil knows that all oxygen atoms, all atoms of a given species, have the same mass or weight. All electrons have the same mass, charge, and spin within an accuracy far greater than can be achieved in man-made things, and this is true for every one of the properties of the known elementary constituents of matter.

In the macroscopic world, in contrast, when we encounter objects that have like properties within measurable limits we at once recognize them as designed by man. As things in nature they are rare or accidental. Coins and paper bills of the same value, automobiles of the same make, and all machinery from an assembly line belong to this category. But being designed by man implies that there is intelligence behind them. Should we not make a similar assumption, are we not compelled to make it, with respect to the fundamental entities of atomic and nuclear physics? But the intelligence behind them was not that of man!

The last of the three idealist philosophers I wish to introduce is Immanuel Kant. He requires little discussion because my own theory of knowledge, contained in *The Nature of Physical Reality* and *Einstein's Space and Van Gogh's Sky,* is based on his epistemology. Some of it is repeated in connection with figure 1 of chapter 4 in this book. Kant emphasizes the sporadic, unordered, unconnected, capricious nature of our immediate sense impressions (my primary or P-experiences). They must be regularized by what he calls categories. This process is equivalent to the transition from my P-plane via rules of correspondence to constructs and their subjection to the principles of verification.

A brief explanation of this strange terminology should perhaps be given at this point. Empirical knowledge arises in a unique way, which may be described somewhat crudely but graphically in terms of certain diagrams. The mind, which is thus far undefined, is affected by sensations, which are a very special kind of experience connecting the mind with the "external world." I shall locate pictorially all sensations on a surface, a plane, which then separates the external world from the mind. Sensations are thus the primary experiences, the protocols, the "prehensions," to use Whitehead's term, which link the mind with the world. The prevalence of the letter P induced me to call the totality of sensations the P-plane.

Sensations alone, however, do not constitute knowledge. The seen color blue needs to be interpreted, usually by means of measurements, in order to become objective, the same, for all observers. These measurements are "operational definitions," more precisely, relations or connections between immediate perceptions and concepts, for example, the blue I see and the wave length measured. Our ordinary language does not distinguish them. Measurements are important members of a class of relations between P-experiences and concepts, defining the latter. These relations constitute part of what will be called the C-field, the field of concepts. But as will appear later, most concepts are actually defined by the way in which reason links them to immediate observations; hence the "rules of correspondence," my name for the P-C relations, in a sense create or construct the concepts. For this reason I shall occasionally call them "constructs." Finally, an observable is a construct like blue or a set of constructs like blue, massive and spherical which defines an external object. The term observable means that whatever it refers to originates in observations.

Kant occasionally uses the Greek term *noumona* for our constructs, in contradistinction to *phenomena* for our P. To him sense data are regularized by categories that bring data under concepts. This gives rise to organized knowledge. "Concepts without factual content," wrote Kant, "are empty; data without concepts are blind. Therefore it is equally necessary to make our concepts sensuous, i.e., to add to them their object in intuition, as it is to make our intuitions intelligible, i.e., to bring them under concepts. These two powers or faculties cannot exchange their functions. The understanding cannot see. The senses cannot think. By their union only can knowledge be produced."

All through Kant's work, chiefly his *Critique of Pure Reason,* one senses the conviction that what is ultimately regarded as real begins with subjective elements and is regularized by the human mind through the use of rational principles. Objective reality relies on interpretation and has its origin within consciousness.

Thus from the standpoint of ontology, the theory of being (in contradistinction to epistemology), an object is not what it seems to be. Its properties are in large part shaped by the percipient subject. The "thing in itself" (Kant's phrase for ultimate being but confused by some writers with his *noumena,* our verified constructs), the true ontological essence, is not knowable by man. This last point deserves emphasis and will occupy our attention once more later.

[handwritten margin note: transcendental vs empirical ego]

Similarly, the ego we come to know is not the "ego-in-itself." This cannot be known in essence either.

Yet we want to know! The faculty allowing us, indeed forcing us, to soar above to natural confines of experience Kant calls "pure reason." This faculty leads to the ideas of pure reason and these are the soul, the universe, and God.

Kant examines these three ideas in his "dialectic analytic" and discusses the contradictions the various proofs of their existence involve. In his *"Antinomies of Reason"* he discusses infinity and finds several logical flaws in the widely accepted proofs for the existence of God.

I conclude by attempting to aid the reader who wishes to study Kant's writings, which are at times difficult to comprehend because of his strange and at time contradictory terminology. Discussion has continued about the meaning of the terms phenomenon, noumenon, transcendental object, and thing-in-itself. The interpretation that underlies the foregoing discourse is this:

Phenomenon: a set of sensory data, a primary (P) experience.

Noumenon: an objective interpretation suggested by data but not necessarily one that corresponds to a particular phenomenon; a construct before it is verified.

Transcendental object: the verified construct corresponding to a particular phenomenon. *(distinguish from transcendent object —)*

Thing-in-itself: the unknowable factor behind experience which *[thing-in-itself]* accounts in a mysterious way for the thus-ness of particular objects.

Chapter 1

Connections between the Physical
and the Living World

It is still widely believed that a complete knowledge of physics, chemistry, and biology will ultimately explain the phenomena of life and account for consciousness and the mind. The latter are said to "reduce" to the former when all details are understood. Reductionism is the philosophy that affirms this view. Its simplest form is materialism, the doctrine asserting that all human experience is ultimately understandable in terms relating to the physics of matter, more specifically the theories of prequantum physics. But the analysis of numerous examples drawn from mathematics and physics leads to a rejection of reducibility in the usual sense as a general guiding principle even in those simple branches of science. My earlier publications[1] replaced reductionism with a principle that may be called transcendence with compatibility. To illustrate the meaning of this phrase in the most elementary way without repeating the elaborate considerations of my previous publications, the reader's attention will here be called to a few basic paradigms: the relation between two- and three-dimensional geometry and the relation between Newtonian mechanics and thermodynamics. In each instance the latter theory contains observables (volume, temperature) that have no meaning in the former; they transcend its domain but are compatible with the observables encountered in it. The reader who feels that the possibility of explaining volume and temperature in terms of areas and speeds of individual molecules means reduction should be reminded that in more complicated instances even this formal relation, this explicability, does not exist: in that sense Maxwell's equations, which involve the concept of a radiation field in empty space, do not reduce to Coulomb's law, which requires electric charges to produce the field. Maxwell's equations expand Coulomb's law but are compatible with it, indeed imply it. The psychologist who tries to explain his subject in terms of physics and chemistry commits the same error as the physicist who attempts to explain Maxwell's equations in terms of Coulomb's law.[2]

The change in terminology and in point of view I am proposing is also suggested, indeed enforced, by more general philosophic considerations. Reduction implies that new knowledge embroiders the old, that there is a core of verities, not all known at a given time, to be sure, which grows and becomes more complex as science advances, but grows from the same old roots. This contractive implication tends to inhibit the kinds of radical novelties that recently emerged in physical and genetic sciences, novelties that were in fact held back by the reductive predisposition.

What happened is far more appropriately described by abandoning the contractive view of reductionism and focusing on the novel ideas that accompany the expansion of knowledge. This is what my new term—transcendence with compatibility—is intended to suggest. Transcendence is the essential feature, and what was formerly called reduction now recedes into the obvious logical requirement of compatibility.

In turning our attention toward the phenomena of life we shall heed this lesson: to expect reducibility, that is, a mere extension of the observables and laws of physics or, more precisely, the laws regulating the behavior of ordinary matter, would contradict even what we found in analyzing the various domains of the inorganic realm. But we do expect compatibility. We must look for novel kinds of observables (in the larger sense defined in note 1) that must not contradict those appearing in our previous examples but need not apply to them, any more than temperature applies to a single molecule. In other

words, we do not assume the observables encountered thus far
to be sufficient as we proceed to the realm of the living.

I intend, however, to make our approach slowly, one step at
a time.

Among the distinguishing features of biology we encounter
organization of a variety of sorts. The first step toward organization is order, something simpler than organization because it
may be static, whereas organization usually implies order increasing in time, or at any rate a more elaborate sort of
regularity or regularization than the term order implies.

The concepts of order and, as we shall see later, of information are stepping-stones from the inanimate to the living world,
for they are present in both. Let us here consider order. It has
two aspects: first, a large one, which expresses itself in the
functioning of inviolable laws of nature, in the absence of
miracles. Let it be noted here that the term miracle is not as
clear and definite as most of us believe. If it is a breach in the
laws of nature, then its recognition requires a full knowledge of
the laws of nature,[3] and this is clearly not at hand. Telepathy
and clairvoyance[3] are often regarded as miracles, but if a
scientist were asked what laws they contradict his answer would
be unsatisfactory. The best he could do is to affirm that at
present he knows of no laws that permit them, which still leaves
their miraculous character in doubt. The sudden emergence of a
dense star in the sky near us would surely be regarded as a
miracle by nearly everyone, although it might not contradict
any known law of nature. For if it had the proper ratio of mass
to radius its total energy could be zero, and so could its total
linear and angular momentum. In fact, the creation of the
entire universe out of nothing may not be a miracle, as I have
elsewhere noted. Other known laws of nature would forbid
occurrences we would regard as possible: in view of what has
been said about quantum mechanics (see note 1), a particle
having as small a mass as an electron could never remain fixed
at a definite spot unless a very strong force held it there.

Yet the existence of laws of nature has been a source of awe and wonder to thoughtful people throughout the ages. Genesis gives a beautiful account of their origin which is often over-looked even by theologians. This example was also given else-where and I ask the reader's indulgence for repeating it here, for it deserves more emphasis and wider appreciation than the literature accords it. At the end of the great Flood Yahweh appears before Noah under the rainbow, pledging: "I will not again curse the ground any more for man's sake . . . While the earth remaineth, seed-time and harvest, and cold and heat, and summer and winter, and day and night shall not cease . . . I do set my bow in the clouds . . . and I will look upon it that I may remember the everlasting covenant between God and every living creature . . ."

This is a second story of creation, in many respects more important than the seven-day story that precedes it. The theo- logian Schleiermacher spoke of the existence of laws of nature as the greatest miracle, before which all those reported in the Bible fade into insignificance.

The second aspect of order refers to an arrangement of parts, as exemplified by the periodic table of the elements, crystal structure, the arrangement of cells in an organism, and the structure of DNA. Let us briefly review how current theory accounts for this arrangement.

In physics the origin of order is very easily identified. The simple features of quantum mechanics and Heisenberg's and Schrödinger's theories satisfactorily deal with the "one-body problem," the behavior of a single particle in the microworld, for example, the single electron we encounter in the hydrogen atom. These theories allow the electron to move in specific "orbits" of increasingly higher energy. The word, "orbit," still used for simplicity, must of course not be taken literally. It refers to a certain probability distribution for the electron's position which has the spatial shape of a diffuse ring or shell about the proton. Each orbit is characterized by quantum numbers, and for each orbit the energy is possessed, not latent.[4] So is the total angular momentum. The higher the energy, and this means the larger the orbit, the greater becomes the variety of quantum numbers that identify the orbit. The lowest-energy orbit, the so-called ground state of hydrogen, has two quantum numbers, the first excited state 8, the next one 18—in fact, the nth state has $2n^2$ quantum numbers. All this can be shown by solving the one-particle Schrödinger equation for an electron attracted by a positively charged nucleus.

Let us now consider, in addition to hydrogen, some of the heavier elements, which have as nuclei, aside from electrically neutral neutrons, multiples of the proton charge and correspondingly many electrons "moving" about them. The theory described thus far would place every additional electron in the first, or lowest, orbit because it is most economical with respect to energy. But this is not what is found. Nature accommodates only 2 electrons in the lowest orbit. Lithium, for instance, the element with 3 electrons, has 2 in the lowest and 1 in the next higher orbit. Sodium, with its 11 electrons, features 2 in the lowest orbit, 8 in the next, and 1 in the third orbit. In other words, there can only be as many electrons in an orbit as the orbit has quantum numbers; every electron "wants" its own set of quantum numbers. This is a simple, not very profound statement of the Pauli exclusion principle: no 2 electrons can have the same quantum numbers.

Before pursuing the matter further, I should make two points. First, the principle is meaningless and could never have been foreseen from a study of the one-body problem. There is compatibility between the many- and the one-body problem, but somehow a new observable, as yet unnamed, enters the scene when many particles are present. We encounter the same kind of one-way continuity of explanation—compatibility—that we found in passing from Newtonian mechanics to thermodynamics.

The second point is a peculiar, more philosophical one. Suppose we have a Li-ion, that is, a nucleus with three protons (and 4 neutrons, which exert no force on an electron) surrounded by two electrons. Now we add a third electron. We know that it is not the electrostatic repulsion that keeps it from joining the other two. Nor do we know of any dynamic agency that is responsible for its disposition to avoid them. Somehow it "knows" the other two are there and seeks its own private orbit. The word "knows" is not wholly out of place because there is no physical agency that accounts for the known facts. One is almost tempted to say that some sort of ESP governs the behavior of electrons.

But what is the new observable that must be invoked and subjected to a novel law in order to explain what happens, to explain the third electron's "knowledge" in the example of Li? To introduce it I must first note a glaring defect in my simple statement of the exclusion principle given above. That statement refers only to a single atom, for in two lithium atoms we have two electrons occupying states with identical quantum numbers. In this instance, to say that one atom "knows" that the other one is there will not work, for strange things happen when the two atoms approach each other. They then lose their identity and interact in ways that lead straight into chemistry. But there is a correct, albeit more abstract mathematical way in which the exclusion principle can be expressed without loopholes or exceptions. It involves a new observable called *symmetry*. To explain it I return to the quantum mechanical state function called ψ. It contains the coordinates of all constituents composing the system whose state it describes. Let us label the electrons contained in a collection of atoms $e_1, e_2 \ldots e_n$, their coordinates $x_1, x_2 \ldots x_n$.[5] The state function ψ may then be written as $\psi(x_1, x_2 \ldots x_n)$. This function will usually change its form when two of its x-coordinates are exchanged. Among the effects of interchanging two x's are two that are simple and interesting. The first effect is one in which ψ retains its form, the second one in which it merely changes its sign. In the first case ψ is said to be symmetric (with respect to an exchange of coordinates), in the second it is called antisymmetric. The common case in which ψ is totally altered is called unsymmetric. The simplest examples of symmetric, antisymmetric, and unsymmetric functions (of two variables) are, respectively, $\psi = x_1 + x_2$, $\psi = x_1 - x_2$, and $\psi = x_1 + 2x_2$.

With this understanding we can state the exclusion principle in its correct and precise form: Every $\psi(x_1, x_2 \ldots x_n)$ usable in quantum mechanics must be either symmetric or antisymmetric. What a strange law of nature! The exchange of coordinates has nothing to do with an actual switch of positions among the entitites to which the coordinates refer. And finally, nature differentiates between those entitites. If they are electrons, for instance, ψ must be antisymmetric; if they are photons, symmetric. Unsymmetric state functions do not seem to occur. The symmetry principle shares with the cruder formulation of exclusion the fact that it loses its hold on single particles; $\psi(x_1)$ has no symmetry, any more than a single atom has temperature, hence it leaves the laws governing single quantum particles intact.

But what a strange "observable" is symmetry! The name observable is justified, of course, only in the wider sense previously discussed:[6] it is a construct, in fact a quantity, within the C-field at a symbolic place rather distant from the P-plane of direct sensory experience but connected with it first by certain constitutive definitions that terminate on P via rules of correspondence. That the observable is abstract should no longer concern us, for we are dealing with the microcosm where visualizations only lead us astray.

The laws of symmetry are axiomatic. We cannot at present point to any deeper principle from which they can be derived. They have an aspect of mathematical simplicity and beauty, but we do not know their origin any more than we know the origin of Newton's law of gravitation.

The laws of symmetry do, however, open up vistas of an enormous scope, for every kind of order in the molar universe seems to be a consequence of them. Their potency is manifest in large areas of physics, all of chemistry, and therefore much of biology.

As has already been indicated, the exclusion principle accounts for atomic structure. Without this structure, every atom would collapse into a positive nucleus surrounded by an unorganized mass of negative charges. There would be very little distinction between different atoms, and their interactions—the forces between them—would be much alike and too small to account for known facts.

Mendeleev discovered the periodic table of elements as an empirical fact. The table lacked an explanation for 60 years, even though it made possible the successful prediction of unknown elements. Pauli's exclusion principle allowed the table to be understood in one fell swoop. Associated with this understanding was the discovery of valence: the forces that unite atoms into molecules, whose strength differs greatly in different instances, are connected with the quantum numbers that antisymmetry assigns to the outermost atomic electrons. Atoms that do not combine into molecules have been shown on the basis of the exclusion principle to exert repulsive forces at close distances.

Not only valence forces but even the weaker intermolecular forces that cause adhesion of substances, capillarity, and surface tension have their origin in the antisymmetry principle coupled with the symmetry-controlled forces arising from the arrangement of the outer electrons.

These latter forces, together with valence forces, are responsible for the regular arrangement of atoms and molecules in a crystal. This spatial order, as in the geometric symmetry of the carbon atoms in a diamond, has its origin in the antisymmetry of ψ. A piece of steel can be a magnet because of it.

It should be evident that the principle under discussion known as Pauli's principle, is responsible for every form of order in physics and for all of chemistry, inorganic as well as organic. It is true that its detailed application to complicated molecules, such as those encountered in organic chemistry, is often beyond the mathematical ability of the scientist and even the computer; but the experience that has been gained in such efforts gives clear evidence of its general validity.

I have not as yet spoken of biology. Insofar as this science relies on physics and chemistry it utilizes the principle of symmetry implicitly. One specific rather interesting instance of the use of Pauli's principle relates to genetics: the process of replication of the double helix, DNA. For a correct reproduction of a living cell the proper constituents of a chain, the nucleotides thymine and adenine and guanine and cytosine must come together to form pairs in the new chain, the double helix; otherwise a mutation results. The forces bringing these constituents together are known to be hydrogen bonds, whose origin can be traced to the principle of symmetry.

Before leaving this subject, I wish once more to impress on the reader (1) the vast range of application and the immense fruitfulness of a law regulating the observable called symmetry and (2) its abstractness, its lack of reference to any of the ordinary properties of matter. The distinguished biophysicist Harold Morowitz calls symmetry *noetic,* a term derived from the Greek word νους, which means mind or consciousness.

There is indeed something quasi-mental, nonphysical, about it. Earlier I used the phrase "one electron knows what the others are doing." The amazing fact is that we do not know of any physical influence that effects the avoidance by one electron of an already occupied atomic state. Furthermore, there is no evidence whatsoever that the adjustment to the principle requires time. We may have here a true case of action at a distance, a case that incidentally does not contradict the principle of relativity because there is no energy or mass transfer involved.

The discovery and application of Pauli's exclusion principle is perhaps the most remarkable example of transcendent but compatible elaboration. One wonders whether a further, as yet unknown, noetic principle may not be needed to account for the facts of life and of consciousness.

Information is the second measure of order and organization that I mentioned as a possible stepping-stone to the living world. This is not the place to discuss the theory of information and its quantifiability in terms of the logarithm of the probability of an event. The concept is an extremely useful one and has led to great advances in the techniques of communication. In its application it makes no reference to conscious knowledge—the number of bits of information contained in a given message is independent of whether the message is known. Noteworthy, however, is the fact that information is defined as negative entropy. A law of inanimate nature claims that (in closed or isolated systems) entropy never decreases. Only in processes related to living systems, which are always open, does it decrease. Hence it may be observed that information, also called negentropy, which clearly increases as time goes on, displays the same tendency as life.

Furthermore, while the theory of information says nothing about consciousness, consciousness would be meaningless without information. It implies consciousness, opens a door to it, measures what goes into it—but somehow stops at the entrance. One wonders whether a future elaboration of information theory may not throw some light on the hitherto obscure nature of consciousness.

Frederic Vester,[7] important European biologist and TV commentator, writes concerning the information resident in a living cell: "Does a cell know to which part of the body it belongs? Yes, it most likely does. But that is a problem which has not yet been solved." He calls it "intercellular communication," leaving its nature unspecified. The physicist, on reading this, is strongly reminded of the communictions between electrons via the exclusion principle.

The present form of information theory is not adequate to deal with the mind. If, for instance, our mind received two messages, one of n_1 bits, the other of n_2 bits, reason could draw conclusions not contained in the two separate messages; the total information produced has more than $n_1 + n_2$ bits.[8] I also note that this would lead to a decrease in entropy even if the mind is an isolated system. Such a violation of the second law of thermodynamics is presumably not possible for a physical organism, which decreases its entropy only at the expense of its surroundings.

Chapter 2

Evolution

Darwin's great work, the *Origin of Species,* established the foundation for the theory of evolution. It describes the development of increasingly complex organisms and of the innumerable living species in terms of two fundamental ideas: random genetic propagation and survival of the fittest. The main philosophic issue, and the one that has stimulated heated controversy ever since 1859, is hidden in the word "random."

The controversy has not abated in spite of two remarkable discoveries that illuminate and verify Darwin's basic thesis of genetic propagation: the discovery of Mendel's laws and the unraveling of the structure of DNA together with its crucial role in transmitting genetic information.

Darwin's theory of evolution relies heavily on chance, unmitigated chance. Even the emergence of man is said to be largely an accident. Taken literally in its original formulation it would justify the statement by G. G. Simpson, who claims in *The Meaning of Evolution* (New Haven: Yale University Press, 1949) that "man is the result of a purposeless and materialistic process that did not have him in mind. He was not planned."

Simpson's book deserves further comment. It is one of the best presentations of the geological facts of evolution and genetics as they were known at the time of its publication. In some of its fundamental assumptions, however, it is evasive, and its philosophic and physical premises are sometimes biased, sometimes contradictory to modern theories.

To do full justice to Simpson's view I should state that the above quotation is followed a little later in the same paragraph by the statement: "It is, however, a gross misinterpretation to say that he [man] is *just* an accident or *nothing but* an animal" (italics mine). The reason why he is not an accident, why his evolution is not merely a matter of chance, is the nonrandom factor of adaptation. The mechanism of adaptation is natural selection, which has this basis: "in every population some individuals have more offspring than others. This obvious fact automatically accounts for the possibility of evolutionary change." Adaptation is therefore a form of Darwin's good old "survival of the fittest." This, Simpson emphasizes, provides a measure of orientation to the evolutionary process, but he cautions the reader not to confuse adaptation with purpose or any of its synonyms, like *elan vital,* cellular consciousness, Berg's nomogenesis, Osborn's aristogenesis, Smuts's holism, Rosa's hologenesis, Driesch's entelechy, or du Nouy's telefinality.

Simpson does, however, believe in strict causation of the classical mechanistic kind. Aside from the untenability of this view he seems to be unaware of the following difficulty it entails, if it is true. The most pregnant formulation of classical causality, also called determinism, involves Laplace's famous demon, an imaginary being capable of solving the most complex mathematical equations. Such a being could, if it knew the state of the universe at any moment (for example, at the beginning of astronomical time), calculate all subsequent states. It could therefore have predicted the entire process of evolution with absolute precision. There is, of course, no need to postulate the demon. Laplace's statement is an impressive way of saying that the initial state of the universe, its temporary boundary condition, predetermined all future states. Hence Simpson's advocacy of strict determinism, the usual ingredient of classical mechanics and of what he terms materialism, commits him to the consequence of predetermination, or even preformation in the biological sense. But this conclusion is not espoused in the treatise under discussion; most of its contents speak against it. Adaptation would also be predetermined.

The modern physical thesis, which had already replaced classical causality at the time of publication of *The Meaning of Evolution*, is the philosophical basis of the quantum theory that has meanwhile forced science to discard determinism. As was shown in *Einstein's Space and Van Gogh's Sky* (New York: Macmillan, 1982) by LeShan and myself, events in the microcosm are not determined by Laplace's fomula: they are individually unpredictable. The uncertainty principle defines the range of phenomena that constitute the microcosm, and in the present discussion of human freedom the constituents of biological processes and hence the elements of evolutions belong to this realm. Its adoption would rescue Simpson from the dilemma of predetermination, but it would have introduced elements of unforeseeable complexity with which his book fails to deal.

Simpson's rejection of metaphysics as a necessary accompaniment of science poses a further serious philosophical problem, for this rejection causes him to speak in certain passages like an extreme empiricist, an attitude he clearly does not wish to adopt. But his view that the facts of science generate metaphysical principles puts the cart before the horse: metaphysical principles both precede and are verified by every full-fledged science. *Einstein's Space and Van Gogh's Sky* (part 2) has dealt with metaphysical principles; a more extensive discussion may be found in my earlier book, *The Nature of Physical Reality* (Woodbridge, Conn.: Ox Box Press, 1977). Faith, which according to Simpson is said to be justified but is placed outside of science, is an essential part of its domain. These two peculiarities—adoption of classical causality and the mistaken notion of the needlessness of metaphysics—are disturbing ingredients of Simpson's informative book.

A defect from the point of view of modern physics is the exclusive reliance on what is called materialism or mechanism, two terms that seem to designate the same doctrine. Materialism is closely connected and occasionally identified with what Simpson calls causalism. This connection is indeed proper, for every materialistic philosophy involves Laplacian determinism in the sense outlined above. But causalism, as we have seen, has been radically modified by quantum theory and is no longer valid in the sense required by Simpson's argument. It is therefore somewhat disturbing to read on page 274 of his book that "once causalism is abandoned there are no limitations on the flights of the imagination and there are about as many separate vitalist and finalist theories as there have been vitalists and finalists." To analyze this issue a little further, let us separate materialism and causality and assume that Simpson, in the just quoted statement, means materialism when he uses the word causalism. This raises the issue of the status of materialism in current physics.

The basic tenet of materialism is that all reality consists of matter, a view fairly tolerable at the end of the last century, when Haeckel proclaimed it forcefully. But much has happened in the meantime that discredits this view. The demise of a material ether, the presumed carrier of light waves, destroyed the vital core of the doctrine. Radiation was clearly seen to be nonmaterial, and when it was later shown to consist of so-called photons, which under many physical conditions are discrete, nobody was allowed to regard them as particles of matter. Since then, numerous nonmaterial entities have invaded the realm of physical reality; they are usually called fields; they often carry energy but rarely matter in the usual sense. If the reader sees a loophole in this assertion and argues that, after all, Einstein proved the equivalence of energy and matter, and matter *is* therefore universal, I counter that some fields, such as the probability field of quantum mechanics, carry neither energy nor matter.

Today it is even difficult to maintain that entities that were originally regarded as material—the so-called "particles" of atomic physics—retain the essential characteristics of matter. As explained in *Einstein's Space and Van Gogh's Sky* the so-called particles do not retain the visual qualities of the constituents of the molar world, such as color, size, even position and velocity. In fact, their nature is highly abstract;

they are constructs of an unfamiliar kind. The verdict is simple: materialism in Haeckel's or Simpson's sense is dead.

Reflections of this kind prompt us to comment on a strange feature of the history of science. The early scientists both of Europe and the Far East did not regard the nature of the human mind as a problem but advanced numerous conjectures regarding the nature of the material world (*vide* the atomic theories of Leucippus, Democritus, and Kanada or the philosophy of Parmenides). The materialists of the last century, on the contrary, felt they knew all about matter but practically nothing of the mind. Indeed, many of them, and even some today, denied its existence. To characterize the present situation one is forced to say that both agencies, mind and matter, are incompletely known and present fascinating problems.

Simpson's philosophy of evolution distinguishes three positions: materialism, vitalism, and finalism. He wishes to reject the last two, as do some other biologists. We now see, however, that we are forced to confront them. Vitalism in its strictest sense (see Hans Driesch, *The Science and Philosophy of the Organism*), postulates a "vital force," an entity playing the same role as physical forces and presumably having the same physical dimension. This view cannot be rejected on a priori grounds, but an appeal to it is useless so long as a vital force has not been discovered and analyzed. If the meaning of the term *force* is extended, if the vital force is endowed with nonphysical properties, its postulation becomes precarious and lacks, at present at least, persuasive scientific appeal.

We are therefore left with finalism, the philosophy that assumes some sort of purpose (*telos*) to be active in the processes of evolution. This last contingency will be considered later in these pages.

So much for a philosophical critique of Simpson's impressive book. He concludes by noting a feature that has caused some readers to wonder. Like many biologists, he casts man in a unique role. Man alone is said to be able to communicate, to have a language, to feel responsibility, to reason. It is true that the evolution of the brain has reached in man a most complex form. But the question is often asked by thoughtful observers of animals, indeed by some psychologists, whether many species do not communicate in rational ways, whether they have not developed a language, perhaps a largely nonvocal one, by which they convey their thoughts, feelings, intentions, and purposes. One thinks of homing pigeons, of bees, of dolphins, of the evident understanding between domestic animals and their owners, or of the sorrowing pigeon that will not move from the dead body of its mate. If all this is to be explained by invocation of instinct rather than reason, one might wish to ask where and when instinct ceases and reason begins. This author's private belief is that the term *instinct* is very poorly defined and its use by psychologists covers a deficiency of basic understanding. It is certainly as vague as Jung's subconscious.

The appearance of the concept of chance in a fundamental theory is by no means unique; we observe its action in most sciences, indeed in all those that feature epistemic feedback, an effect of knowledge (measurement) on "being" (see note 3). Quantum mechanics, as we have seen, not only manages to live with chance but even thrives on it.

There are, however, two important differences between the role of probability in quantum mechanics and in Darwinism. One difference is that quantum mechanical probabilities can be computed in an a priori manner, and their values have been verified through innumerable measurements. This is not true in the theory of evolution, where the probabilities involved are related to certain conjectured chemical processes, starting with the formation of organic molecules in the primordial slime and ending with highly complex reactions in present living organisms, such as photosynthesis and metabolism. While attempts have been made to assign probabilities known from reaction rates to the various chemical processes involved in the evolution of the exceedingly numerous species existing today and then to use those probabilities to estimate the length of time in which the highest species could have developed, the results have on the whole been extremely disappointing: chance alone would require a vastly longer period than the 15 billion years our universe is believed to have existed. This does not mean it is impossible; it is merely an unusual and unexpected series of events.

The second difference in the character of probabilities in the two fields is this: in quantum mechanics the probabilities important in the microcosm congeal to certainties, to deterministic observables in the molar realm. There seems to be no clear analogue to this "asymptotically regular" behavior in evolutionary chance—although, as will be seen below, there are tendencies in that direction today.

Much of the work dealing with neo-Darwinism is somewhat technical and will be reviewed here only briefly. An excellent philosophical review of many of its phases has been given by Ervin Laszlo.[4] Specific references are to the works of Waddington and Koestler,[5] Sinnott,[6] and Lillie.[7]

The reader chiefly interested in biology would profit from these books. Especially striking are certain points of Waddington and Koestler. Koestler, for instance, comments on the idea of homology of organs, which is usually explained by assuming that similar genes are transmitted from a common ancestor. On page 133 and thereafter, however, he shows that experiments on drosophila contradict this theory, and he reaches the conclusion that recombinations of genes involves coordination "according to some overall plan." I too am led to similar inferences.

Koestler also discusses homology, the theory that similar organic structures have a common origin. The arm of a man and the wing of a bird, for example, developed from the same forbear and were transmitted by the same gene complex, varied by mutations and environmental selection. This theory was seen to fail in experiments with drosophila conducted by Morgan. He found that if a pure line of flies bearing the "eyeless" form of the gene is inbred, then after several generations there emerge specimens with perfectly formed eyes, a result evidently of the cooperation of different genes.

Koestler's[5] remarks on this phenomenon appear appropriate and convincing. He writes:

> The traditional explanation of this remarkable phenomenon is that the other members of the gene-complex have been re-shuffled and re-combined in such a way that they deputise for the missing normal eye-forming genes. Now re-reshuffling, as every poker player knows, is a randomising process. No biologist would be so perverse as to suggest that the new insect-eye evolved by pure chance, thus repeating within a few generations an evolutionary process which took hundreds of millions of years. Nor does the concept of natural selection provide the slightest help in this case. The recombination of genes to deputise for the missing gene(s) must have been co-ordinated according to some overall plan . . .

Many biologists may prefer an alternative and more recent explanation of the drosophila findings in terms of what they call reverse mutations. I find that Koestler's interpretation includes these modern views. Other books containing equally important arguments are: A. Koestler, *The Roots of Coincidence* (London: Hutchinson, 1972), and A. Koestler and J. R. Smythies, eds., *Beyond Reductionism* (London: Hutchinson, 1969).

Many interesting particulars may be found in the papers by Waddington and in the books by the geneticist Sinnott. Lamarckism (inheritance of willfully acquired characteristics), which would put directive pointers on chance, seems to be generally discredited, even though some recent developments have the effect of partially reinstating it. Waddington's views tend in that direction. He emphasizes that complex organic systems usually exhibit a kind of stability he calls homeorhesis, a word intended to denote that what is stabilized is not a constant value of a given quantity, as in homeostasis, "but a particular course of change in time. If something happens to alter a homeostatic system the control mechanisms do not bring it back to where it would normally have got at some later time." In simple terms the system ignores aberrant deviations and somehow reaches a preset goal. A stabilized goal-directed time trajectory, which Waddington places among the most important features of developing biological systems, he calls a *chreod,* contraction of the Greek words, *chre,* fated or necessary, and *hodos,* path. Clearly a purposive element here enters the scene. Waddington[5] also subjects the whole question of randomness in evolution to careful scrutiny. Here are some significant comments that I take the liberty of quoting at length.

> There are two major factors which reduce the importance of the randomness of mutations. In the first place, evolution produces systems which allow for genetic material to be changed not only by random mutations, but also by processes of recombination between existing genotypes. In recombination whole blocks of DNA become shuffled around, and this is a very different process *from changing one or a few nucleotides as occurs in mutation.*

> The second factor which mitigates the effects of randomness in mutation is the increasing complexity of the epigenetic processes by which the genotype is developed into a phenotype. This means that the effects of any given gene mutation will be affected by interactions with a great many other genes. As we have seen, epigenetic processes tend to be chreodic, that is to say to have certain stability characteristics. These may be sufficient to buffer out the effects of a good many gene mutations, which will then bring about no noticeable change in the end products of development; or if the genes do produce an effect this will be as much dependent on the stability characteristics of the epigenetic system as on the nature of the gene mutation. Many different mutations may in fact cause the same alteration to the phenotype, and that is another way of saying that, if natural selection is pressing for some particular alteration of a phenotype, there may be many different genetic ways of producing it. In such highly evolved complex organisms the randomness of the basic gene mutations is, as it were, buried deep in the complexity. It is rather like the randomness of the shape of the pebbles which form the aggregate of the concrete out of which a bridge has been built. It remains true enough to

say that the ultimate units, the pebbles in the concrete, or the genes in the organisms, have been produced by random processes, but this is almost irrelevant to the engineering of the bridge.

And finally, to quote Waddington again, "genetic assimilation makes it possible for evolution to exploit . . . the cleverness of physiological reactions to stressful situations." He thus adds to Darwin's random selection and survival of the fittest a new principle, which he calls genetic assimilation.

Arthur Koestler, one of the distinguished contributors to *Beyond Reductionism*, adds interesting comments, which heighten the significance of this new element, to these remarks. In his book *The Case of the Midwife Toad*[8] he clearly expresses the feeling that Darwinism is incomplete, that it needs implementation by purposive principles hitherto unknown.

Laszlo, who adopts the mildly teleological view of Waddington, states the case as follows:

> The interaction of the environment with the genotype and of the latter with the developmental "epigenetic space" and through it with the "genotype space" provides the dynamics of a complex adaptive process whereby populations of organism *creatively* respond to changing conditions in their environment, evolve internal constraints expressed in the genotype and in behavior patterns, and become more able to cope with relevant environmental fluctuations than previous organic forms.

Evidently, something remotely resembling purpose has entered the evolutionary stream. Evolution is stabilized by features resembling the Lamarckian transmission of acquired characteristics, but in a more sophisticated way.

"Epigenetic space," a concept foreign to Darwinism, is Waddington's term for the range of action of evolving chreods.

We now turn to E. W. Sinnott, an outstanding geneticist who had a profound interest in philosophy and an expert knowledge of it. He speaks of Darwinism as natural selection from random variations, which amounts to a combination of two ideas: random genetic propagation and survival of the fittest. I quote from his *Matter, Mind and Man*[6]:

Perhaps the most difficult problem in development to explain is how thousands of genes, each affecting a particular process, show such exquisite coordination that a precise embryological program is carried through to its specific end. How this is done is difficult to imagine. Doubtless we shall learn much more about such developmental problems in the future, but the fact that so little progress has yet been made, in comparison with the vast amount achieved in problems of metabolism and physiology, suggests that our mechanical ideas may be too naive and that something fundamental may remain to be discovered about biological processes.

The mechanist will suggest that the capacity for growth regulation is simply another character which has been developed by natural selection from random variations and has reached its present high perfection through a long evolutionary process.

The difficulty of this explanation is that it explains too much. Many cases of regenerative ability in nature would be called upon so rarely that they could hardly be affected by selection. One must imagine that plants and animals have suffered an almost infinite variety of mutilations and in great numbers, if selection were to be effective in developing their ability to restore all kinds of structures. Furthermore, this ability is often manifest in cases which could never have arisen in nature but only through manipulation in the laboratory.

There is another objection to the idea that selection is responsible for developmental regulations. Their chief visible expressions are the very precise *forms* which the structures of animals and plants display. Some of these are of survival value but many, such as the particular patterns of protozoa and diatoms, or the precise wing venation by which each of hundreds of species of closely related flies can be distinguished, are almost certainly not "life-and-death" characters.

Here Sinnott's remarks might be amplified by a layman's observation, culminating in the question: "Why is there so much beauty in nature?" We do not believe that beauty is only in the eye of the beholder. There are objective features underlying at least some experiences of beauty, such as the frequency ratios of the notes of a major chord, symmetry of geometric forms, or the aesthetic appeal of juxtaposed complementary colors. None of these has survival value, but all are prevalent in nature in a measure hardly compatible with chance. We marvel at the song of the birds, the color scheme of flowers (do insects have a sense of aesthetics?), of birds' feathers, and at the incomparable beauty of a fallen maple leaf, its deep red coloring, its blue veins, and its golden edges. Are these qualities useful for survival when the leaf is about to decay?

I feel it necessary to quote Sinnott once more when he says, "The universe makes sense only on the assumption that there is a creative purpose behind it that is akin to mind." He quotes Eddington: "Shuffling can have inorganic causes but sorting into an organized pattern is the prerogative of mind." In sum, then, "The early conclusion, reached in the first flush of enthusiasm over Darwin's great hypothesis, that *all traits of an organism have resulted by means of natural selection and are therefore of value to it, is now recognized as too general*" (italics mine).

A vague recognition of "directedness," which is implied by Sinnott's remarks, had led previous investigators to propose theories that are now generally abandoned. Hans Driesch[9] postulated an "entelechy," a special agency. Entelechy is not a physical observable like energy, nor does it violate the laws of thermodynamics. Driesch's conception of it, however, seems as vague as it was in Aristotle, from whom he borrowed the term. But it designates a factor that impresses form on matter, actuality on the merely potential, and with Driesch it also underlies man's psychical processes. Others speculated about a vital force, advocating a theory called vitalism, but this view now has very few adherents.

Ralph Lillie[10] has this to say:

> . . . the psychical factor offsets the physical tendency toward uniformity and dissipation; and under its directive influence, essentially teleological, the routine physicochemical processes are guided and coordinated in such a way as to build up and

maintain the special biological organization—which in the purely physical sense is so completely "improbable."

Increasingly, the appeal to a psychic factor for the maintenance of life, often for regularization of chance, is voiced by biologists. Sinnott goes beyond that, as do many others, claiming that "the *universe* [italics mine] makes sense only on the assumption that there is a creative purpose behind it that is akin to mind." Biologists are joining many philosophers, who are usually more explicit in avowing the overall need of a psychic element. Two further quotations, typical of a growing sentiment in philosophic quarters, may illustrate this trend.

C. E. M. Joad[11] concludes: "I am thus led to postulate the presence in the universe of a . . . principle of change which . . . is known to the biologist as life, to the psychologist as mind, and to myself as the stream of consciousness which constitutes my being."

Alois Wenzl[12] goes even further, universalizing the biologist's search by claiming:

> Nature includes a will to live (*Lebenswillen*), i.e., a spatio-temporal lawfulness which may be called a realization of archetypes by individualization of ideas . . . Were we to ask for a carrier for the order of things we would arrive at "personified" nature, in which there inheres this striving and finding of the way, either in the form of pantheism—*deus sive nature*—or of panentheism, a god immanent in the world or a transcendental divine creator.

In retrospect, then, we find that modern theory of evolution, and biology as a whole, confront us with an unsolved problem, a problem likely to involve the concepts of mind, consciousness, and purpose. Max Delbrück, a physicist who received a Nobel Prize in biology, hinted in the proper direction[13] when he said:

> Instead of aiming from the molecular physics end at the whole of the phenomena exhibited by the living cell, we now expect to find natural limits to this approach, and thereby implicitly new

virgin territories in which laws may hold which involve new concepts and which are only loosely related to those of physics.

In other words, the solution can probably not be foreseen from the explanatory modes of present-day physical science. We must expect compatibility with, but transcendent elaboration on physical science. The transition we are facing may be like that from Newtonian physics to thermodynamics or from one-particle quantum mechanics to the exclusion principle. The new observables may be meaningless, useless, or unnecessary for the physical universe, from which they cannot be seen.

As a result of this survey of the recent biological literature in the fields of evolution, neurophysiology, and studies of the mind I am led to make the following observation. There is a clear tendency among numerous distinguished writers to avoid every explanation not strictly grounded in the immanent view of mechanism, not to say materialism. Appeal to presumed "nonphysical" theories is unfashionable and arouses suspicion. The most important advances in the field, especially in genetics, have indeed been largely explicable in terms of complex but conventional organic chemistry. Biologists have not yet experienced the transcendental leaps beyond customary ideas which Einstein and Heisenberg forced physicists to take.

Many of these biologists, in trying to understand evolution, are still wedded to the old-fashioned but highly enigmatic notion of chance.[14] Almost all of them seem to feel, however, that the original Darwinian concept (which is probably falsely ascribed to him) needs some qualification, needs an invocation of some directedness, perhaps even goal-directedness, but they are embarrassed and unwilling to call it purpose or design.

Most scientists generally reject the term *vitalism,* and it should be rejected in its original form, in which it tried to introduce a new vital agency, a force or an energy, into science. But in a more general sense, a sense in which an understanding of life might require nonphysical principles of its own, it need not be excluded categorically. What strikes this author as amazing is the perplexing and perhaps revelatory verbal camouflage that is often employed to define and inject something somehow directive, a quasi-purpose, into the process of evolution. I cite here Driesch's *entelechy,* a word Aristotle boldly employed to define purpose. Driesch, however, refuses to accept that definition, claiming it to mean "potentiality made actual." *Emergence* is used by many authors, but seemingly never in the sense of transcendence, except perhaps by the philosopher Broad. Waddington's *epigenetics* ("execution of genetic instructions") try to conceal purpose. *Homeostasis* is used by Monod, one of the strongest advocates of the sufficiency of chance; he also speaks of "ampliation of DNA" and thereby implies at least a semblance of purpose. Others mean by homeostasis the capacity to adapt to circumstances. *Preformation,* the view that an egg cell contains the preformed organism, is now discarded by all (this is a valid rejection, based on convincing negative evidence). Medawar used the terms *progressiveness, holism* (that is, the view that all living systems tend to form highly integrated and indivisible entities), and even *teleonomy,* which is teleology mitigated.

Nomogenesis (L. S. Berg) is evolution determined by law, but not a law addressing the future. Dobzhanski, one of the most authoritative writers, had the courage to speak of "internal teleology," but he conceives it as "imposed upon the evolutionary process by the blind and dumb engineer, natural selection." Laszlo uses the term *biperspectivism* to introduce a mental aspect into the living, conscious process.

Only a minority of authors explicitly avow the action of purpose in evolution and all processes of life. Most notable among them are probably Teilhard de Chardin, who uses the impressive phrase "paroxism of harmaonized complexity," and De Nouy, who doubles the emphasis on purpose by his term *telefinality.* Yet even in the popular literature there seems to appear some tolerance of the idea of purpose. As is well known, Jean Baptiste de Lamarck opposed a theory like Darwin's in 1809 by asserting and attempting to prove that acquired characteristics could be inherited. This could hardly be explained by an appeal to chance and was viewed as an injection of a mild form of purpose into the evolutionary process. Until recently, Lamarck was regarded as the "bad boy" by geneticists, and when his view later surfaced in the Russian literature it was condemned along with other Marxist claims.

Now the *Journal Science Digest* (March 1981) has this to say:

> Right now, in a laboratory in Toronto, Dr. Edward J. Steele is working on experiments that, while not actually debunking Darwin, might prove Lamarck right. In collaboration with Dr. Reginald M. Gorczynski, Steele has demonstrated that induced immunity in mice can be inherited by their offspring. This would be comparable to a child's being protected against smallpox through the mother's vaccination.

> The British journal *Nature* commented, "It is not easy to offer an alternative mechanism for the transmission of tolerance which is any more credible than the Lamarckian one favoured by Steele and Gorczynski."

There were times when evolution was regarded as too worldly a subject to be taught in schools, as contradicting established religion. Its present state, enhanced by the last amazing discoveries, induces admiration and awe; our tentative understanding of the complexity of an organism—the detailed self-replication of cells, the incomprehensible repair of damage, the constant, almost incredible, daily replacement of atoms that preserves form—appear more miraculous than any physical process we know. Thus it seems that evolution, far from being foreign to the kind of feeling that induces religious attitudes and concerns, is uniquely suited to create them.

Our society seems at present to be drawn back into a debate reminiscent of the Tennessee monkey trial. Some religious fanatics feel that there is a contrast between the theory of evolution and divine creation; they advocate that since religion is barred from the curriculum of public schools, evolution should not be taught either. In response to this tendency I feel compelled to quote a friend now deceased, one of the most distinguished biologists of the last half century, Theodosius Dobzhansky, who wrote: "Evolution is God's method of creation. The cosmic, biological, and cultural evolutions are ultimately parts of a single creative process."[15]

The preceding comments on the problems posed by evolution would be incomplete if they did not also recognize the highly important work of Sir John Eccles,[16] whose Gifford Lectures were published after the foregoing text was written. His authority adds greatly to the view I am about to develop. While Eccles does not directly invoke a purposive agency in the development of life, he regards the origin of life as a mystery and marvels at "the manner in which biological evolution was constrained [sic!] through its waywardness to lead eventually to Homo sapiens, and finally to the origin of each individual conscious self." And further: "In this process we can see repeatedly how plasticity was cherished though at the cost of immediate success and at the risk of extinction of our evolutionary line. It has to be recognized how tenuous was that line of evolution that led to us." To me this implies that if the development of man were entirely a result of chance it would be an accident, a sequence of events so unlikely that the statistician would regard its occurrence as absurd. And furthermore, because of its single occurrence, the statistician could never prove its chance character, not even by adding any of the half-baked replacements of purpose that have been suggested. And a resort to an infinite length of time would hardly help the statistician.[17] Eccles finally quotes C. S. Sherrington, one of his predecessors as Gifford Lecturer (Cambridge University Press, 1940), from "Man on His Nature," who says in relation to his last point:

> Does it not seem strange that an unreasoning planet, without set purpose and not knowing how to set about it has done this thing to an extent surpassingly more than man has? It is to be remembered that Earth's periods of time have been of a different order from man's and her scale of operations of a different order, and that man's cunning in this respect dates but from yesterday. Yet, we agree, it does seem strange.

Chapter 3

The Mind–Body Problem:
Monism, Dualism, or Pluralism?

Most philosophers and many scientists dealing with the mind-body problem classify their views as either monistic or dualistic. I wish to show that this is an anachronism that can no longer be tolerated in the science in which it arose: physics. One of the most careful classifications of existing theories attempting to relate the mental to the physical is found in a paper by Bunge,[1] who distinguishes five kinds of psychoneural monism and five kinds of psychoneural dualism. On the basis of conventionally cogent evidence he declares himself a monist, more particularly an emergentist materialist. In this chapter we analyze the mind-body problem a little further, conferring special attention upon developments in recent physics.

Like all queries into the nature of elements or modes of existence, the distinction between monism and pluralism is an ontological one, and ontological questions, dissociated from epistemology, can only be answered on the basis of faith. And affirmation of faith can only be subjected to logical, not empirical, scrutiny—which is highly indecisive and leaves many mutually contradictory faiths alive. Hence we must rely on epistemology and its recent refinements, the methods of successful science, for evidence relevant to our problem.

There can be no question that all our knowledge, both about the world and ourselves, arises within consciousness, our own or someone else's. And science is, after all, systematic knowledge about the world and ourselves. As I have explained elsewhere, to be systematic knowledge must satisfy two impore

We must then ask: Is
onstructs? An answer,
, and it somehow still
lherents of this view
rt is fragmentary but
vill someday prove it
f the mind-brain iden-
onism, has now disap-
sm would still remain.
for the fact that an
osophers and indeed
in the field of neurol-
ity theory, seemingly
oncerning the relation
ized as transcendence
w understanding will
sional reasons will be
nan) mind other than
the brain in a manner

errington wrote in the
action of the Nervous
t of two fundamental
nherent improbability

the Mind (Princeton
otes Sherrington and
for the assumption of
ce based on Penfield's
udy and treatment of
e problem under dis-
n independent agency,
e of the brain's action.
ontext Penfield cites
e messenger" to con-
omparison, suggesting

tant classes of principles: (1) verification, that is, satisfaction of expectations implied by it (experimental validation) and (2) certain metaphysical principles like consistency, extensibility of the constructional system composing the knowledge, causality, simplicity together with elegance of formulation and probably others which the progress of science will force us to invoke.

The most economical epistemology, and surely the safest, stops at this point and asserts that our knowledge of the world is forever stamped by its origin: made in the mind, hence mental. Even the above-mentioned metaphysical principles are the products of thinking. Verification is a matter of perception, and both are mental acts. Considerations such as these lead to indisputable idealism or epiphenomenalism. Primitive as this philosophy is, it can nevertheless take a slight variety of forms, the extremes being solipsism and Berkeleyan idealism. Neither can be refuted by logical or even scientific considerations.

Why, then, do we reject this view? Essentially because it is noncommittal, unfalsifiable, drab, monistic, but also monotonous. Fundamentally we are repelled by it as we are by a room whose walls are painted in neutral gray; we want variety, true understandable variety, such as walls with rhythmic patterns or walls decorated with pictures. And furthermore, we are not forced to stay within the desert of epiphenomenalism.

I have shown earlier that the observables of science are not *only* perceptions, that scientific constructs are never identical with mental acts even though these are their origin. What intervenes, what separates them, are the rules of correspondence. These may be classified and seen to form several types, such as operational definitions, simple and complex rules, all leading from P into the C field. The most important rule in the present context is reification, which endows a complex of sensations with reality, physical, sensory reality, by fiat, if you please. The epiphenomenalist can shrug this off, saying that, after all, the observables, the constructs, are still mental, still specific phases of my or someone else's consciousness. And he

is right. But his attitude is that of *nil mirari*. His c
why the rules of correspondence leading to the po
external world actually work, why they are so
successful, is not aroused or is artificially suppre

The scientist, however, cannot do this. He tak
of all proper acts of verification as proof of the e
external world, indeed as obviously demanding
outside his mind. And thereby he slips, often unkr
an ontology. Reason alone does not force him t
everything that now surrounds him says "bravo"

At this point a philosopher is tempted to conclu
The scientist gives sufficient weight to the external
although he may have constructed it by rules of re
mental origin, nevertheless emerges as a self-reg
pendent entity. Being coherent and complete, ev
the circumstances of its genesis, the external wor
reality that sets it apart from the mind itself. Henc
ought to call himself a dualist. And if he lived a
Descartes or even later, if his knowledge of physics
to the theories prevalent at the end of the last c
external reality was generally equated with mat
distinct essences would be matter and mind. Their
complementary ingredients of reality, not neces
Cartesian terms of *res extensa* and *res cogitans*, cha
most common scientific ontology today. It is al
fundamental view, the most widespread philosophy
essence of our entire culture, relating to matters
from science. It was, in fact, the essence of con
made even more acceptable by the demands of rel
last three centuries.

And yet, this dualism, while commonly accepte
with a feeling of dissatisfaction. A theory that get
one basic entity is preferable from the point of vie
ity (one of the metaphysical requirements impose
and by modern science) to one that requires two.
alive the hope that some day, through further elabo

includes reference to immaterial fields.
the mind, is consciousness among those
widely shared by biologists, is affirmati
identifies the mind with the brain. A
generally admit that its empirical sup
hope that neurophysiological research
correct. To be sure, the earlier appeal
tity theory, which reduced dualism to
peared, for even if it were adopted plur
This circumstance may be responsib
increasing number of distinguished p
some of the most celebrated research
ogy are discarding the mind-brain id
approaching the acceptance of a thesi
of mind to matter which I have charac
with compatibility. Evidence for this
now be presented. To be specific, pr
given in favor of the existence of a (
and independent of, but interacting w
termed transcendent but compatible

In 1947 Nobel Laureate Sir Charle
foreword to his book *The Integrati*
System:[4] "That our being should co
elements offers, I suppose, no grea
than that it should rest on only one

Wilder Penfield, in *The Mystery*
University Press, 1975), approvingl
then provides further elaborate evid
an independent mind, most of the e
experience as a brain surgeon who
epilepsy were unique and relevant
cussion. He concludes that the mind
can give directions to the brain in ad
The mind carries a *message*. In
Hippocrates, who said, "the brain
sciousness. Elsewhere he uses ano

that the mind programs the brain, which acts as a computer. This analogy may now be out of date, for there is some evidence showing that one computer can program another.

To summarize Penfield's position I shall quote him at length:

> For my own part, after years of striving to explain the mind on the basis of brain action alone, I have come to the conclusion that it is simpler (and far easier to be logical) if one adopts the hypothesis that our being does consist of two fundamental elements. If that is true, it could still be true that energy required comes to the mind during waking hours through the highest brain mechanism [the sensory motor mechanism located in the higher brain stem].
>
> Because it seems to me certain that it will always be quite impossible to explain the mind on the basis of neuronal action within the brain, and because it seems to me that the mind develops and matures independently throughout an individual's life as though it were a continuing element, and because a computer (which the brain is) must be programmed and operated by an agency capable of independent understanding, I am forced to choose the proposition that our being is to be explained on the basis of two fundamental elements. This, to me, offers the greates likelihood of leading us to the final understanding toward which so many stalwart scientists strive.

I conclude this lengthy quotation from the writings of one of the world's outstanding neurophysiologists by citing a brief but significant remark from the same work: "Neurophysiologists will need the help of chemists and physicists in all this, no doubt."

I take the liberty as a physicist of adding two points that modify Penfield's view in some details but leave his essential affirmation unaltered. One concerns his dualism, his claim that there are two elements, brain and mind, or in Cartesian parlance, body and soul. Penfield's statement overlooks the fact that modern physics has added greatly to the Cartesian *res extensa*: As we have seen it is no longer merely matter. The external world now contains numerous *onta*, including a variety of nonmaterial fields with properties wholly different from matter, or from fields sustained by matter (like flow fields of liquids, turbulence fields, and sound waves). We have been forced to realize, as I have pointed out elsewhere, that entities not belonging to the see-touch realm, as, for example, some *onta* of the nuclear and atomic domains, need not have visual properties. One of the most abstract fields of modern physics is the state-vector field or the state-function field of quantum mechanics, a field as real and necessary for an understanding of atomic phenomena as the billiard ball is for the person who uses it in the ordinary realm. I repeat: the substance of physics is no longer single and uniform but multiple yet compatible and coherent. Hence its world view is no longer monistic but pluralistic, and this pluralism is further extended when the mind is added to the constituents of existence.

The second point a physicist is likely to make qualifying Penfield's view concerns his insistence that the mind requires energy for the role it plays as monitor of the brain. Energy, as defined in physics, is the ability to do physical work; transfer of energy involves work. But as I have pointed out,[5] the effect of the mind on the brain or more generally on the body need not require energy of this physical kind; the effect is usually a selection of outcomes of which the body is capable alone in accordance with the principles of quantum mechanics. In the reference cited the reader will find an analysis of the act of conation, but a very similar situation occurs in many other interactions of mind and brain. It should furthermore be noted that there are instances in which the principle of conservation of energy in its customary form does not hold: as examples one could cite the passage of electrons through barriers, where in order to save the conservation principle one would have to introduce a non-sensical negative kinetic energy, or the failure of conservation in virtual physical states which occurs during intervals $\Delta\tau$ so small that $\Delta E \Delta\tau \approx (h/4\pi)$, ΔE being the amount of constancy violation and h Planck's constant. This relation is sometimes used in estimating the width of a spectral line.

Finally, and perhaps most miraculous of all, is that a physical mass can be created out of nothing without contradicting the laws of physics.[6]

These observations would seem to remove even some of the difficulties Penfield occasionally mentions as annoying obstacles to his major view.

The irrelevance of physical energy to the mind, indeed perhaps its failure to possess it, is emphasized and strongly affirmed by Carl Jung.[7] He discusses among other paranormal phenomena the experiments of J. B. Rhine who provides evidence that ESP, which Jung accepts as a possible form of communication, is independent of the distance between sender and receiver, which shows in principle "that the thing in question cannot be a phenomenon of force or energy, for otherwise the distance to be overcome and the diffusion in space would cause a diminution of the effect." This view is further strengthened by the observation that the success of ESP experiments depends strongly on the subject's mental attitude. Lack of interest, doubt of success, and boredom affect the results negatively, while belief in success, positive expectation, enthusiasm entail good results.

In his subsequent discussion of these matters Jung goes perhaps further than necessary, further than many scientists would follow him. For he concludes that the absence of energy in the process of thought transfer puts an end to causal explanation because, he believes, "effect cannot be understood as anything except a phenomenon of energy." This seems to limit the use of the term *effect* too severely, for a mental state, a philosophic view can certainly have an effect on behavior. And as might be expected Jung introduces at this point his well-known argument relating to *synchronicity*. He holds that ESP transmission is instantaneous, sending and receiving are simultaneous; the process itself characterizes the unconscious psyche, activating one of the archetypes that constitute the structure of the collective unconscious. All this, therefore, fits beautifully into Jung's well-known philosophy, but, as will be seen, it does not lead to it compellingly. What it does demonstrate is that the mind cannot be conceived in terms of the physical attributes of matter.

Jung makes another interesting but debatable point. It is generally believed that mental, that is, conscious, processes are tied to the cerebrum and that certain lower centers can affect nothing but reflexes, which are unconscious. Hence insects, which have no cerebrospinal system but only a double chain of ganglia, must be unconscious reflex automata. Yet von Frisch,[8] the well-known investigator of the behavior of bees, made a surprising discovery. Not only do they tell their hive members by means of a peculiar sort of dance that they have found a source of food, but they even indicate its distance and direction. This kind of message is practically identical to information conveyed consciously by human beings; it certainly implies an intentional act. Thus we can no longer attach the attributes of consciousness to our cerebral cortex, since the "inferior" gangliomic system of bees achieves exactly the same result. Where, then, does consciousness reside? The best answer might be: nowhere. The mind is something *sui generis*. The fact that it cannot be located does not worry the modern physicist, for he knows of other onta that defy locatability.

Jung's archetypes and his idea of synchronicity have a great deal to do with the essence of the mind; they support its independence from matter in certain ways. But we shall forgo comment on them here, reserving it for a later chapter in which the possibility of the function of a Universal Mind is examined.

Pauli's part of the joint book with Jung[7] entitled *The Influence of Archetypal Ideas on the Scientific Theories of Kepler* is essentially a detailed study of the contrast between the magical and the rationally scientific elements of Kepler's work. Where Pauli's work touches the mind-body problem it is somewhat inconsistent and vague. He comes closest to a significant statement when he observes that "the only acceptable point of view appears to be the one that recognizes *both* sides of reality—the quantitative and the qualitative, the physical and the psychical—as compatible with each other, and can embrace them simultaneously."

More specific is his attempt to invoke Bohr's correspondence principle in its early, now somewhat whithered, form in which it asserts a "complementarity" between certain observable features of physical *onta,* like electrons or photons, which can display the seemingly contradictory properties of particles and of waves. "It would be most satisfactory of all," Pauli says, "if physics and psyche could be seen as complementary aspects of the same reality." If this were true, however, there could hardly be an interaction between mind and body, which all known evidence requires. But Pauli mellows his position, adding: "We do not yet know, however, whether or not we are here confronted—as surmised by Bohr and other scientists—with a true complementary relation, involving mutual exclusion, in the sense that an exact observation of the physiological processes would result in such an interference with the psychical processes that the latter would become downright inaccessible to observation."

Pauli here alludes to a theory of complementarity introduced by physicists in the early days of quantum mechanics and accepted as reasonable by so distinguished a man as Niels Bohr. It characterized what is called the Copenhagen view and has often been called a dualism, a dualism between waves and particles.

The theory of complementarity took essentially two forms: (1) an electron or a photon is sometimes a particle and sometimes a wave, depending on the conditions under which it is observed, and (2) it is both a particle and a wave and therefore a paradox. These meaningless assertions were made innocuous by giving them a philosophic name: the wave-particle dualism. But philosophy and logic at times pass slowly into the domain of physics, and the dualist thesis still has some force. Indeed C. U. M. Smith concludes his book *The Problem of Life*[9] with a statement suggesting that brain and mind form a dualism similar to the wave-particle dualism in modern physics. It is gradually being recognized by physicists that neither proposition 1 nor 2 is satisfactory. They should be replaced by proposition 3: *electrons and photons are too small to be seen and must therefore not be endowed with visual properties. The mind is intrinsically invisible and therefore equally unsuited for representation by a physical model.* The biblical injunction "Thou shalt not make thyself a graven image" needs to be taken just as seriously by today's science as it was by the early Israelites.

Important contributions to the subject of this chapter are contained in the Gifford Lectures of 1977–78 by Sir John Eccles.[10] Eccles's own view is summarized in a table on page 211 of *The Human Mystery,* where he compares it with four others (radical materialism, parapsychism, epiphenomenalism, and the identity theory) and calls his own view dualist-interactionism. Eccles agrees in all essential respects with the thesis proposed in this treatise. Only the word "dualist" is, as we have seen, misleading because the material world, the world of physics, has taken on multiple ontological facets that do not fit into a single scheme of matter.

The uniqueness of Eccles's work resides in the experimental evidence he provides for the interaction between the human brain and an independent self-conscious mind. It resides in his convincing interpretation of the experiments of Kornhuber.[11] A brief description of them is the following.

A subject is asked to perform a rapid flexion of his index finger. In willing this movement there can be measured electrical potentials over a wide area of the cerebral surface; these are called readiness potentials. They are detected approximately 0.8 seconds before the onset of the muscle action potential, which is the physiological cause of the finger motion. It is assumed that the readiness potential is generated by complex patterns of neuronal discharges that project to the appropriate pyramidal cells of the motor cortex physiologically responsible for finger motion. These facts fall into line in Eccles's explanation: The readiness potential in its wide extent and gradual build-up is the neuronal counterpart of the voluntary command.

"Apparently, at the stage of willing a movement, there is a very wide influence of the self-conscious mind on the patterns of module operation." Thus the hypothesis of an independent mind resolves and redefines the meaning of the long duration of the readiness potential that precedes a voluntary action.

Elsewhere Eccles explains the experiments of Libet[12] which indicate that a direct repetitive stimulation of the somaesthetic cortex results in a conscious experience *earlier* than the physiological accompaniment of the stimulus. "This antedating procedure," Eccles says, "is presumably a strategy that has been learned by the self-consciouss mind." Further evidence and arguments for the independent existence of mind will be found in Eccles's contribution to the book by Popper and Eccles.[13]

Transcendental dualism is the term Eccles assigns to his philosophic view. A physicist, however, aware of the multiple immaterial essences that already populate his field, might prefer to say simply pluralism while still agreeing totally with Eccles's view. But the terminology hardly matters if the facts are understood.

The reader who possesses sufficient patience to read this book to the end may find reason to modify this terminology and return to monism in an abstract sense. For our last chapter argues in favor of a universal mind possessing aspects which unify all experience.

Chapter 4

Toward a Study of Consciousness

In the preceding chapters my approach to the problems under discussion was more or less conventional: Its starting point was for the most part the external world. The philosophically oriented reader will recognize this as a predominantly western trait. Even in dealing with the mind-body problem we merely concluded that the mind is not identical with the brain, which is part of the external world, but interacts with it. Before proceeding further it becomes necessary to ask the most difficult questions: What is the external world? In what sense does it exist? Can it be explained without a mind? To answer these questions requires an excursion into epistemology, into the way we gain knowledge of the world, and into the features that render this knowledge stable, objective, and independent of the mind. This last feature—the independence of the external world from the mind—requires special attention, for it will turn out that this independence is not total or unlimited in any ordinary sense. In the next few pages I shall repeat, in a somewhat modified version, parts of the methodological analysis presented more extensively in *The Nature of Physical Reality* (Ox Bow Press, 1980).[1]

Knowledge of the external world is provided by a process that begins with sensations, perceptions, the kind of mental experiences the philosopher Whitehead called prehensions. We use the word *experience* in a rather general sense, akin to the German *Erlebnis,* in which it denotes any conscious process or state. Perceptions or prehensions are a very special sort of experience, and the way science deals with them differs greatly from its treatment of other phases of consciousness, such as feelings (like joy or sorrow), moods, desires, hopes, memories, intentions, conations, and innumerable others that remain unnamed. The term *awareness* is often used in place of *consciousness, external awareness* in place of *sensation.* I deem it desirable to include this material here in order to show the inadequacy of the standard approach to problems encountered in the study of the mind.

Let me first describe how the mind proceeds from what would seem its most elementary function: sensation, perception, prehension (an experience I have called *primary* and abbreviated by the letter P in previous publications) to the features of the external world. Many writers make a distinction between awareness and self-awareness, the latter being associated with knowledge of the self. This distinction is sometimes regarded as highly important, for the view is held that only man is endowed with the ability to be aware of himself, animals can only be aware of extraneous matters. I have never seen convincing evidence for this claim and refuse to believe it involves a general distinction between all animals and man.

Under circumstances specifiable by certain repeatable components of awareness I see a color associated with a certain place (another ingredient of sensory awareness). I activate my sense of touch and find a hard reaction. Vision informs me that the color is associated with a shape; another touch, a grasp, reveals a strain I call weight or heaviness.

The uniqueness of all these simple experiences is that they repeat themselves on similar occasions, that is, when my mind's totality of awareness is similar or the same. My tendency therefore is to assume some sort of permanence that has fixed itself on my mind.

The same sort of process will already have occurred in connection with experiences that are visually and in a tactile manner close to me: I have become aware of my body.

Then I discover that there are other bodies and finally, through some sort of communication—which need not be as elaborate as language—that they have the same mental experiences as I.

These miracles of repeatability and individual agreement between different minds induce me to ascribe my sensations to permanent external bodies: I have taken the first step into the external world. This passage, which starts "at P" (that is, is initiated by a number of primary experiences), may be termed *reification,* making a thing out of a set of sensations. Obviously, if there were no mind, there could not be reification. In the strictest sense, therefore, mind creates the external world.

There is, however, an important addendum to this observation, for it does not take into account the repeatability of the same act of reification, its identical or at least similar occurrence in other minds. So far as a single mind is concerned the continued identity, the stability, the cohesion among reified P-states are inexplicable, are an aspect of the miracle of existence for which no simple scientific reasoning can account.

For science, reification, the mere introduction of external objects and thereby the establishement of an external world, is not sufficient. Science wants to go beyond elementary principles of order that allow reification; it strives to "understand" the external world and predict its behavior. This goal requires the use of further philosophical procedures and the imposition of rational requirements that will now be outlined.

First we note that sensations, all P's, are purely subjective. There is no way anyone can prove that the color red I see and ascribe to an object is the same red you see, or the distance I perceive between two objects is the same distance you perceive, or that the feeling of hotness in your fingertip dipped in a bath is the same as mine. Comparison of sensations must therefore rely on processes beyond subjective appraisal. Since this is an important matter and has serious consequences for a study of the mind I shall outline the objectifying processes in some detail. Note, however, that the analysis which follows applies only to cognitive experience, the sort of mental activation that occurs primarily in sensation. Such cognitive experience characterizes the sciences. Noncognitive experience is characteristic of and explored in the arts, the humanities, and all ethical and religious concerns and involves feelings and mental acts such as remembering, willing, and certain kinds of analytic reasoning.

P includes all possible perceptions or primary sensations like seeing, hearing, tasting, feeling pressure or pain or heat, and many others, far more numerous than the usual reference to our five senses conveys.

Let me now sketch the method of empirical science, using a few simple physical examples by way of explanation. I feel a pressure on my hand and conclude that a force is exerted on it. I may judge it to be strong or weak, but that estimate is insufficient for science, insufficient for a definition of force. Placing my hand in a bath of water, I experience a sensation of heat; again this subjective sensation is not of direct scientific value. I focus attention on what William James called "the flow of consciousness," and I become aware of the lapse of time. This fleeting sensation, however, does not present a measure of time.

The reason is the subjective character of all P's: There is no way of judging whether your sensation under the same circumstances is the same as mine. Science must somehow eliminate the element of subjectivity.

A second defect of P-experiences from the point of view of science is their variability. Even within my own experience, the same external circumstances may cause me to make a different judgment with respect to intensity. If I place my finger in the same bath of water a second time, it may feel cooler, simply because my finger has become accustomed to the hotness through the previous exposure. A similar uncertainty surrounds the experience of a force on two different occasions as well as my judgment as to the time elapsing between two events. This instability must be removed before concepts like force, temperature, and time can be useful to science.

The third characteristic of these sensations is their qualitative nature. They simply present no aspect that would allow the experiencer to attach a number to the sensation.

Subjectivity, instability, and lack of quantifiability are removed by science in a very specific way. Scientific theory does not involve what we have called P-facts directly.[2] The equations of mechanics do not contain the pressure on my hand, nor the sense of heat in my fingertips, nor the flight of consciousness that amounts to a passage of time. Science converts each of these into an idea that *corresponds* to it, an idea that perhaps unfortunately carries the same name as the sensation itself. This may be illustrated easily as follows.

Whatever presses on my hand can be applied to a dynamometer, an instrument recording force. Instead of my finger, I can place a thermometer into the bath and read its indication. The interval of time to which I have devoted my attention can be recorded on a clock. In every one of these instances a number results, and this number is called the force acting on my hand, the temperature of the bath, and the interval of time. Each of these numerical measures bears the same name as the sensation, force in the first instance, temperature in the second, and time in the third. Yet conceptually, the results of these measurements are entirely different from the sensation to which they correspond. The two—P-fact and measured quantity—are related by what I have called *rules of correspondence*. The philosopher Northrop adopted the present analysis but with a different terminology. He called our rules of correspondence "epistemic correlations." In the cases cited the rules of correspondence are *operational definitions*, a term introduced by the distinguished physicist-philosopher Bridgman. Thus the passage from the feeling in my fingertips to the reading of the thermometer is regulated, or is performed, via a rule of correspondence. And so forth. In the following I shall abbreviate rule of correspondence by the letter R. Clearly, R is the quintessence of a measurement. What it connects, not to say equates, is a P-fact, usually a sensation, and an idea, a concept that in a certain sense has been selected by the scientist. The arbitrariness of the selection will form a topic of discussion in a moment. For the present, however, I recognize that the use of R in all tant classes of principles: (1) verification, that is, satisfaction of expectations implied by it (experimental validation) and (2) certain metaphysical principles like consistency, extensibility of the constructional system composing the knowledge, causality, simplicity together with elegance of formulation and probably others which the progress of science will force us to invoke.

The most economical epistemology, and surely the safest, stops at this point and asserts that our knowledge of the world is forever stamped by its origin: made in the mind, hence mental. Even the above-mentioned metaphysical principles are the products of thinking. Verification is a matter of perception, and both are mental acts. Considerations such as these lead to indisputable idealism or epiphenomenalism. Primitive as this philosophy is, it can nevertheless take a slight variety of forms, the extremes being solipsism and Berkeleyan idealism. Neither can be refuted by logical or even scientific considerations.

Why, then, do we reject this view? Essentially because it is noncommittal, unfalsifiable, drab, monistic, but also monotonous. Fundamentally we are repelled by it as we are by a room whose walls are painted in neutral gray; we want variety, true understandable variety, such as walls with rhythmic patterns or walls decorated with pictures. And furthermore, we are not forced to stay within the desert of epiphenomenalism.

I have shown earlier that the observables of science are not *only* perceptions, that scientific constructs are never identical with mental acts even though these are their origin. What intervenes, what separates them, are the rules of correspondence. These may be classified and seen to form several types, such as operational definitions, simple and complex rules, all leading from P into the C field. The most important rule in the present context is reification, which endows a complex of sensations with reality, physical, sensory reality, by fiat, if you please. The epiphenomenalist can shrug this off, saying that, after all, the observables, the constructs, are still mental, still specific phases of my or someone else's consciousness. And he is right. But his attitude is that of *nil mirari*. His curiosity about why the rules of correspondence leading to the postulation of an external world actually work, why they are so phenomenally successful, is not aroused or is artificially suppressed.

The scientist, however, cannot do this. He takes the success of all proper acts of verification as proof of the existence of an external world, indeed as obviously demanding its existence outside his mind. And thereby he slips, often unknowingly, into an ontology. Reason alone does not force him to do this, but everything that now surrounds him says "bravo" to his stance.

At this point a philosopher is tempted to conclude as follows. The scientist gives sufficient weight to the external world which, although he may have constructed it by rules of reason from its mental origin, nevertheless emerges as a self-regulative, independent entity. Being coherent and complete, even aside from the circumstances of its genesis, the external world takes on a reality that sets it apart from the mind itself. Hence the scientist ought to call himself a dualist. And if he lived at the time of Descartes or even later, if his knowledge of physics were limited to the theories prevalent at the end of the last century, when external reality was generally equated with matter, the two distinct essences would be matter and mind. Their invocation as complementary ingredients of reality, not necessarily in the Cartesian terms of *res extensa* and *res cogitans,* characterizes the most common scientific ontology today. It is also the most fundamental view, the most widespread philosophy forming the essence of our entire culture, relating to matters far removed from science. It was, in fact, the essence of common sense, made even more acceptable by the demands of religion, in the last three centuries.

And yet, this dualism, while commonly accepted, leaves us with a feeling of dissatisfaction. A theory that gets along with one basic entity is preferable from the point of view of simplicity (one of the metaphysical requirements imposed by Occam and by modern science) to one that requires two. This keeps alive the hope that some day, through further elaboration of the sciences exploring the external world, one might find a niche for the mind, presumably in certain parts of the brain and other neural complexes. Hence the prevalent view today is dualistic, but it is pervaded by a hope for and a drive toward materialistic, or even mechanistic, monism.

I now examine this view from the standpoint of modern physics, which allows us to clarify one side of the present body-mind dualism. Perhaps much to the reader's surprise, I do not find the "body," generally conceived as matter, tending toward a merger with the mind; I find it splitting into an increasing variety of essences that are nonmaterial, highly elusive, incomprehensible to "common sense," often incapable of visualization and localization, illustrating Whitehead's "fallacy of simple location."[2] No one is sure at this time whether these essences include the mind, although this hypothesis has been voiced.

The curious difficulty in which science finds itself at this stage is that the scientist who declares himself a monist is unable to point to a single entity in whose sole reality he believes. Certainly, matter and immaterial fields cannot be regarded as one substance or one reality. And the number of fields that are devoid of matter and are substantially unrelated to each other increases rapidly. Nobody can say what consciousness is if viewed as a substance—and dualism means to count irreducible substances or, more precisely, what we have called *onta*.[3]

This means that the physicist, whether or not he includes consciousness in his set of unrelated agencies, can no longer call himself a monist, nor a dualist. If he wishes to preserve the old-style language, he must confess his allegiance to pluralism. My own conclusion is that the old distinction has become superannuated and meaningless.

An important problem, however, remains. Suppose we accept the view that the world of bodies contains a variety of different constituent constructs and ingredients that defy a monistic classification, but we lump them all together and call them *matter,* a term we admit is inappropriate because it includes reference to immaterial fields. We must then ask: Is the mind, is consciousness among those constructs? An answer, widely shared by biologists, is affirmative, and it somehow still identifies the mind with the brain. Adherents of this view generally admit that its empirical support is fragmentary but hope that neurophysiological research will someday prove it correct. To be sure, the earlier appeal of the mind-brain identity theory, which reduced dualism to monism, has now disappeared, for even if it were adopted pluralism would still remain. This circumstance may be responsible for the fact that an increasing number of distinguished philosophers and indeed some of the most celebrated researchers in the field of neurology are discarding the mind-brain identity theory, seemingly approaching the acceptance of a thesis concerning the relation of mind to matter which I have characterized as transcendence with compatibility. Evidence for this new understanding will now be presented. To be specific, professional reasons will be given in favor of the existence of a (human) mind other than and independent of, but interacting with, the brain in a manner termed transcendent but compatible.

In 1947 Nobel Laureate Sir Charles Sherrington wrote in the foreword to his book *The Integrative Action of the Nervous System*:[4] "That our being should consist of two fundamental elements offers, I suppose, no greater inherent improbability than that it should rest on only one."

Wilder Penfield, in *The Mystery of the Mind* (Princeton University Press, 1975), approvingly quotes Sherrington and then provides further elaborate evidence for the assumption of an independent mind, most of the evidence based on Penfield's experience as a brain surgeon whose study and treatment of epilepsy were unique and relevant for the problem under discussion. He concludes that the mind, as an independent agency, can give directions to the brain in advance of the brain's action. The mind carries a *message*. In this context Penfield cites Hippocrates, who said, "the brain is the messenger" to consciousness. Elsewhere he uses another comparison, suggesting these instances achieves (1) objectivity, that is to say, intersubjectivity, sameness for all observers, in place of subjectivity; it introduces (2) stability, for if I repeat the measurement of any of these three quantities under the same conditions I get the same answer. Finally the qualitative aspect of the sensation, of the P-fact, is removed, quantification has been achieved and the results of this quantification, the numbers arrived at by operational definitions, take their place in the equations of science and in its theories. In order to distinguish the two *relata,* the starting point and the end point of a rule of correspondence, we speak of the first as a *P-fact,* of the second as a *construct.* The meaning of this word is practically identical with *concept.* I choose it to imply the performance of a mental and often a physical act in its genesis, an act that is more than a mere conception. The term *construct* suggests a measure of creativity, of participation on the part of the scientist, and this was intended, for, as we shall see, the passage from P to the field of constructs is not wholly unique but subject to selection under rational principles.

To explain and elaborate this important point, to expose the constructive, indeed to some extent arbitrary, character of the rules of correspondence, I will again consider an example. In connection with time measurement, the R involved the use of a clock. But there are many devices that can function as a clock: a pendulum, the sun, the stars, the vibrations of a quartz crystal, atomic and nuclear vibrations. Thus we speak of a pendulum clock, a mechanical clock, the solar clock, an atomic clock, and a nuclear clock, and what they yield is called pendulum time, clock time, solar time, sidereal time, atomic time, and nuclear time. Now these times, these measures that correspond to the flight of consciousness in our mind, do not completely agree in their numerical values. Pendulum time is subject to the force of gravity as it acts on the surface of the earth. Mechanical time is affected by the temperature and other properties of the clock mechanism, solar time and sidereal time differ greatly from each other and also from all the other times we have cited.

Atomic and nuclear times are the least susceptible to variation and are thus more reliable in the ordinary sense than any of the others. Reliability and independence of external influences clearly cause the scientist to prefer the latter kinds of time, but this reliability attaches to solar time and more particularly to stellar time as well. Why, then, is it that the time indicated by atomic and nuclear vibrations is in general preferred by the physicist to the other definitions of time? On careful examination one finds a rather curious answer to this question. Variability, or dependability, is a relative matter; one can only say that sidereal time differs from solar time, that atomic time differs from pendulum time, but which of these is to be chosen must depend on considerations more basic than those presented by empirical circumstances. The criterion for preference is not variability, but a law, a basic law of nature, that takes on a particularly simple form when one choice is made and a more complex form for other choices. The law of nature in this instance is Newton's first law of motion, which claims that bodies not subject to a force move equal distances in equal times. This law becomes increasingly true as we pass from the first named measures of time to the last named, from pendulum time or solar time to atomic time or nuclear time. Clearly, then, a choice is made in the application of a rule of correspondence, the choice being that which leads to the simplest, the most convenient, or aesthetically the most appealing, law of nature.

The same thing is true for all other constructs. To illustrate further I choose one last example. A dynamometer ordinarily contains a spring, and the quantitative measure of a force is taken to be proportional to the extension or compression of the spring caused by the force to be quantified. If the spring is properly chosen, this definition of force leads to another very simple law of nature—to Newton's second law—which claims that force is equal to mass times acceleration. Mass and acceleration likewise have operational definitions, which, however, we shall not trouble at this point to discuss. The preceding examples illustrate that rules of correspondence, in this case operational definitions, are subject to choice and that this choice is governed by principles of reason, in the foregoing instances chiefly the idea of simplicity.

A simple diagram (figure 1a) that has been used in previous publications clarifies and symbolizes this seemingly complex methodology. I think of the mind as a vast domain of conscious activity that at our present stage of knowledge is difficult to define. P-experiences form its boundary with the external world. They may be conceived to lie on a vertical plane, the P-plane of figure 1, which is meant to be a projection on the plane of the paper and therefore appears as a line. To the right of it are all other possible ingredients, all other components of consciousness, its other properties, or, to use a term prevalent in physics, its other observables, such as thoughts and feelings.

A point on the P-plane denotes a sensation, a perception, a P-fact. The region to the left of all P symbolizes the external world. The double lines are our rules of correspondence. They connect a P-fact with its construct (C): the sensation of hotness with the measured temperature, the flight of consciousness with measured time, and so on. A construct of this simple type (simple means "close to the P-plane") denotes a property or an observable that carries a numerical value. In constructing the external world several such C's, such properties, are assigned to a body, or a particle, or some other more abstract or elaborate system, which is the carrier of C's. An atom or a light beam or three-dimensional space might be such a system. In our diagram, therefore, several C's are connected by single lines to a C, which denotes the system, the carrier of observables C whose lines extend to it. In general, single lines denote logical relations, which either define new constructs or establish relations between them.

The figure must of course be extended indefinitely up and down; I have drawn only a small part of it.

The double lines in the diagram are of different lengths. This is meant to indicate that some constructs, like temperature and time in the discussion above, have very simple operational

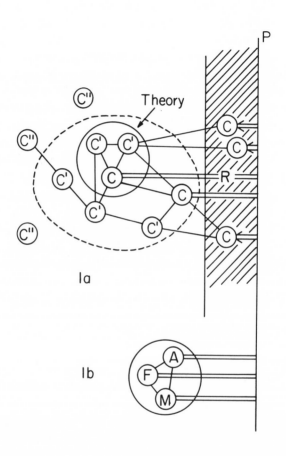

Figure 1

definitions, or, speaking figuratively, they lie close to the P-plane. This is true for most mechanical constructs or quantities—often also called variables or properties—such as mass, weight, speed, and acceleration. But every science also contains constructs that have a more complicated definition, are more difficult to visualize, and may be said to lie at a greater distance from the P-plane. Among them are work, kinetic and potential energy, action; entropy, electrical charge, magnetic field, strength, electrical potential, current strength; light intensity; and in economics such constructs as gross national product, national wealth, index or rate of inflation. In some of the latter instances, the lack of clarity with respect to the choice of R's is a defect from the point of view of exact science.

Some circles marked C' in my figure are also connected by single lines. These circles represent the makings of laws of nature, in which operationally defined constructs always end up, provided the rules of correspondence are properly chosen. To give an example: having defined mass, acceleration, and force, we find that these three quantities are related by a threefold relation, namely, Newton's second law, $F = MA$. Figure 1b is its symbolic representation. The constructs A, M, and F are acceleration, mass, and force. Each is connected by a double line, an operational definition, to P, and the single lines imply that any two of these constructs determine the value of the third. This is typical of all constructs no matter how far they lie from the P-plane. Constructs (for example, C'') that do not have single lines connecting them with other constructs are not useful in science. They are called insular or peninsular; they are sometimes introduced in the hope that with the advance of scientific knowledge they will enter into combination with other operationally defined constructs. The dotted enclosure, which contains simply connected Cs and C's, represents a theory.

The act of reification fits into the scheme of figure 1 but with certain modifications. The rules taking us from a set of sensations to an external object are not operational definitions; they form a class so general and simple that they often fail to be recognized. Here is an illustration. As I look before me "I see a desk." The words in quotation marks are a metaphor. The desk is not a P-fact; seeing it is not a simple P-experience. My immediate awareness is of a brown color, a certain shape, a solid substance, and numerous other sensory qualities. Each quality is capable of an operational definition, but having experienced these sensations so often and so regularly, I do not trouble to invoke these definitions. There is further the remarkable fact that the same sensations occur every time I look in the same direction. I therefore pass, for the most part unwittingly, from the recurring complex of sensations to a single construct, desk, which I endow with permanence, with presence, even when I am not looking at it, with an interior and numerous other properties that reveal and confirm themselves after the passage from the set of sensations to the construct has been performed. This passage, which is in essence a rule of correspondence leading from a complex of P-facts to a construct belonging to the class of external objects, I have called reification. It is an important door opening on the physical world, and we locate the "things" (constructs!) to which it leads intuitively very close to the P-plane. But it is important to realize that they do not lie on the plane.

This may seem like an unreasonable claim, which will be rejected by the realist philosopher. The fact is, however, that the construct desk is not strictly a part of my sensations. For what I see and touch does not have an interior revealing itself without further manipulations; I am not aware of the molecules and atoms of which I believe it to consist; its surface is not rectangular: it appears as a trapezoid from where I sit. In fact, it changes its shape as I move. But if I measure the length of its edges I find them to be the same, and this is true no matter from what position the measurements are made. Thus, in assigning the rectangular shape to the surface of my desk, I am invoking a rational principle called invariance, a form of simplicity compatible with all observed P-facts. All this is combined in the rule of correspondence (R) called reification, and it is the rule that fills the world with innumerable external objects. In view of such considerations A. Eddington in his *Nature of the Physical World* distinguishes two desks: the uninterpreted complex of sensations (the positivist's desk) and the reified (the physicist's) desk.

Figuratively speaking, these are constructs immediately adjacent to the P-plane. Because of their abundance we have not drawn them in figure 1 but have drawn a shaded region next to the P-plane that is meant to be their locus. These constructs must, however, be recognized as being there, for nearly every scientific rule of correspondence assumes their presence, starts from them, and moves our inquiry further to the left into the C-field. There is perhaps no harm in saying that they form an extended P-plane. But we must never forget that external objects are strictly constructs, connected to P by the rule we call reification. That rule takes us from the threshold of consciousness, the P-experiences, into the external world.

We have thus far encountered two types of R: the operational definition and the act called reification. This does not exhaust their classification. There are quantitative constructs that require a more complicated passage from P into C. Examples in physics are density and specific heat. In order to determine and define density we must first introduce the idea of mass, then of volume. Then we define density as mass per unit volume. To determine specific heat one must first find the heat content of a given substance and divide it by its mass. Similar derived quantities appear in all other sciences. The chemical concept of valency does not yield to a single operational definition. It involves theoretical ingredients such as the structure of an atom and goes on from there. Examples of "derived quantities" are extremely numerous; all sciences abound with them. In terms of our diagram, they arise as follows: Starting at the P-plane one first defines operationally a number of simpler constructs. These are then joined with an eye to usefulness or simplicity into combinations that lead to such ideas as the ones we have just mentioned. In a certain symbolic sense, these constructs, though in principle all operationally definable, lie farther away from the P-plane than those with which we have dealt previously. They are related to P perhaps not by a single R but by a rule extended by further definitions. Symbolically we place these constructs within the C-field, but farther away from P and connected with it not by individual double lines but by double lines extending to other constructs that are then combined by single lines. If we wish a name for this latter more complex R, we might simply call it an extended rule.

Further study of the rules of correspondence would lead to the exposition of many other interesting complexities, features indispensible for the complete epistemology of science; but these will not concern us here. For more detailed discussions see *The Nature of Physical Reality*.

Some constructs in every science are not operationally definable in a direct way. Every C' in the figure represents one of these. To name a few, a body in general, an electron, a positron, or in fact any object as distinct from a property is a scientific entity that does not acquire its meaning from an operational definition alone. Its "properties," such as the charge of an electron or its mass, can be defined operationally, but in order to define the electron itself, it will ultimately be necessary for us to say: the electron is that "entity" (*on*) which possesses such and such operationally defined quantities. The carrier of these quantities—the entity specified in terms of its observable, operationally definable quantities—will be called a *system*. Thus, in general, systems have quantities, that is, observables define them *constitutively*; the quantities themselves, however, are always capable of operational definitions. We can therefore classify the important entities that appear in any science into two types: (1) systems that are capable only of constitutive definitions and (2) quantities or observables that are capable of both operational and constitutive definitions. Type 2 requires perhaps one further comment. We have shown that a quantity like force does possess an operational definition, involving a procedure that employs a dynamometer. We might also, however, define force constitutively by saying that it is mass times acceleration. That the two definitions agree is what makes science successful and applicable.

Having discussed how consciousness invades the realm of constructs, it may be well to say a word about the use of constructs after they have been defined in order to explain that part of scientific methodology allowing movement in the C-field. The question arises: How does one arrive at laws of nature, which are logical combinations of constructs? In my figure the laws of nature would correspond to a set of connected constructs such as the one indicated by L, which stands for law of nature. The validity of the combinations termed *laws* is of course dependent on their agreement with what happens on the P-plane. In other words, it must be possible to pass from the law via the single lines and finally via the double lines to the P-plane and encounter the P-facts that the law farther to the left permits us to predict. This process is called verification of the law. But a study of the history of science shows that in the original formation of the laws of nature, other concerns play an important role. As explained much more fully in *The Nature of Physical Reality,* the tentative search for laws proceeds in accordance with some very general guidelines called methodological or metaphysical principles, which are imposed on the character and structure of these laws. At this point I need only mention them: the laws of physics, the laws of every empirical science, are sought in harmony with the requirements of simplicity (Occam's razor), stability, extensibility, causality, and finally elegance of formulation. Much more should be said about these important governing strategies of science. They can never be ignored, for their effects are extremely important. The reader desiring further information is referred to the last mentioned book.

A question may arise as to the origin of this overarching dynasty of principles. Where do they come from? The answer is simple. While they are imposed on man's search for knowledge, they are not in any sense a priori, for they have evolved slowly in the history of science. The list given here may not be complete or conclusive, for in the future newer categories, newer methodological principles, particularly one closely tied to the "beauty" of mathematical equations, may well appear. The latter is already on the horizon. An aspect of it is the concept of invariance, which is increasingly employed in discriminating between true and false theories.

I have dealt perhaps too briefly with one important aspect of science called testing or confirming a theory. A single passage from the plane of percepts into the field of constructs does not satisfy the scientist, even if the passage is in conformity with all guiding metaphysical principles. He requires a return from a certain theory (area of connected C's) to the P-plane by applying the same rules but arriving at different P's than the ones from which he started. And this process of reversal must succeed a sufficient number of times. Thus, full establishment of scientific reality requires a number of passages from P into the C-field and back again. Such an excursion is known as confirmation of a theory, an act that confers reality on all constructs it passes on its way.

This ends my review of the methodology of science, of what might be called the human creation of the external world. We started at the edge of consciousness, the protocol (P) experiences, went from there into the realm of constructs subject to human creation and capable of logical combinations in accordance with metaphysical principles, and concluded with the conviction that what the field of constructs contains and what is referable back to the P-plane and confirmed in the act of comparison is real in the usual sensory or physical sense.

I have emphasized that quantification which leads to the use of numbers and thereby of the ordinary types of mathematics, is carried into the scheme by rules of correspondence; it is an important feature in the practice of every science that leads to knowledge of the external world.

But consciousness, as we have seen, contains more than sensations, more than the aspect I have called P. We must now turn to the major problem of seeing whether there is a scheme of handling the noncognitive part of the mind—the aspects other than those anchored in P—in a manner as successfully as physical and biological scientists have dealt with the cognitive part.

To give an example of the use of regulative principles, called metaphysical in my discussion, I add a few comments from psychology concerning invariance. The field of psychophysics presents a great number of so-called sensory illusions. The figure of a man drawn of equal size in several instances against a background showing perspective seems to grow larger in the distance. A coin does not appear circular unless it is held with its plane perpendicular to the line of vision; sun and moon appear larger near the horizon; there are many instances of misleading perspective. In all of these instances a variety of P-features is ignored and replaced by something that under proper circumstances appears as P but is usually not present in individual sensory appearances. The confusing variety of P's is ignored against one simple invariant, one that is selected for the purpose of translation into the C-field.

We should feel entitled to say, "All our knowledge of the world originates within the mind." This is at once the most comprehensive, universal, safe and indisputable statement that can be made. But it prompts us to ask two questions. One is: Would there be a world if minds performing the process previously outlined, the process of "constructing" (or reconstructing) reality, did not exist? This is one of the difficult problems of ontology. According to Kant the branch of philosophy called metaphysics—the subject with which we are dealing here—has two branches: epistemology and ontology. I feel, largely convinced by Kant and following his reasoning, that ontology must rely on faith and cannot be dealt with by the methods defining science. The question, however, is not meaningless. I tend to answer it negatively, but mainly for reasons that will appear in later chapters of the book.

The other question is: Does our mind reflect the features of an existing world? Here my answer is a qualified yes. As is already apparent to the reader, we cannot accept the naive materialistic claim usually implied by the affirmation, nor do we countenance a simple Cartesian dualism. But we must recognize that there are certain constraints on the mind, the constraints exercised in the choice of rules of correspondence, and furthermore the guiding metaphysical principles that are active in the formulation of theories (such as simplicity, confirmation by reference to the P-plane, invariance, and beauty). To be sure, our mind has apparently originated these principles, but they nevertheless put their imprint on what is regarded as real. In other words, our construction, and hence our recognition of reality, of the world, depends on compulsive features that are not of our arbitrary choice.

It is true, as has been noted, that these guiding principles are not given by the mind in an absolute and unchangeable way. As they change, the face of reality changes. It is even possible, indeed likely, that they are different in different fields of experience, that necessary alterations in them lead to alternate forms of reality. As an example I cite the principle of causality, which was discussed in *Einstein's Space and Van Gogh's Sky* (Macmillan, 1982).

These inherent constraints on the manner in which the mind constructs reality confer special attributes on the results of its construction, on the external world. But the mind does not create and recognize a world with features *arbitrarily* imposed by the constructing agency, the mind.

For this reason the word "reflect" in the formulation of our question is hardly proper. There are principles that guide the mind, principles not totally of its choice, which are active in the process leading to our knowledge of the world, which, however, is not *independently* preexisting. In this context, wherein we assign greater responsibility to the creative power of the mind than is ordinarily accepted, I remind the reader of one supportive aspect of previous considerations. In reviewing recent developments in the theory of evolution we have already encountered grave difficulties with the monistic view, which asserts the primacy of the external world and the derivative nature of consciousness. I merely call attention once more to the need for assuming purpose in the world. And purpose, orientation toward aims, is a typically mental trait.

Before concluding this chapter I wish to emphasize one important point. The methodology of physical science, its total epistemology, makes use of only one aspect, one observable of the mind: sensation, the "observable" we have denoted as P. Feelings, memories, moods, desires, hopes, volitions, and many other mental states have not entered the scene. For them, we have found as yet no universally accepted operational definitions, no satisfactory rules of correspondence. There are numerous proposals, such as one that asks an individual to rate the intensity of his feeling, his interest in a specific event, or the strength of a wish on a scale of 100 and proceeds using the quantitative rules and the metaphysical principles of established science. Here lies the main problem of psychology, social science, and related disciplines.

As a rule we sidestep the problem in ordinary discourse. To describe mental states we tend to employ metaphors relating to the external world, like "a burning desire," "boiling rage," a "quiet state of mind." A large collection of these phrases appears in *Einstein's Space and Van Gogh's Sky*. I take the liberty of repeating them here: high spirit, feeling low, solid character, stiff attitude, bright outlook, dark gloom, glowing pride, ebullient joy, high ideals, low character, deep thought, high ambition, firm or frozen conviction, open or closed mind, calm disposition, sharp reasoning, dull mind, soft heart, shaking faith, black mood, iron will, bright hope or expectation, unshakable faith, sparkling humor, red anger, yellow timidity, and green envy. I note here merely that the use of these phrases is symbolic; it does not permit the kind of quantification, made possible by operational definitions, our previous R's, and it sets the methodology of psychology, sociology, and economics far apart from the physical sciences.

I conclude this chapter by repeating one major point: The aspects of consciousness, its "observables," cannot be treated by ordinary scientific methods. New approaches must be found.

Chapter 5

Extension of Scientific Epistemology Required for a Study of the Mind

Figure 1 in the preceding chapter was used to illustrate the way in which the scientist establishes physical, including sensory,[1] reality. Its main constituents are P (perceptory) experiences, rules of correspondence (R), and constructs (C). The figure must of course be thought of as three dimensional, extending an unspecified distance into and out of the plane of the paper. Hence I spoke of the P-plane, not the P-line. The mind is not included in this diagram, except through the P-plane, which symbolizes its outer border, where it makes contact with the roots of physical reality. The shaded region to the left of P is the locus of sensory constructs, of things formulated by reification.

A recent book by Popper and Eccles[2] contains an interesting diagram which, by a slight distortion and simplification, can be drawn as an extension of figure 1. The latter neglects the distinction between Popper's worlds 1 and 3, both of which are constituents of our C-field. The result is figure 2, an elaboration of figure 1 turned through 90 degrees.

The P-plane is here drawn as a horizontal line. Above it, in my symbolism, lies the mind, below it the field of constructs. The shaded area below P, marked S, represents sensory reality, the realm of objects related to P by simple reification; it is represented by very short double-line arrows. The longer arrows connecting P with various constructs (C) are more elaborate rules of correspondence; the shorter ones represent simple operational definitions. The longest ones define more abstract and more complex observables and/or things. Note also that

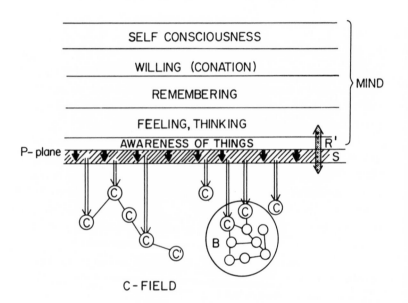

C - FIELD

Figure 2

some constructs are not directly connected with the P-plane; the single lines connecting them are rational, nonempirical, in the sense that they cannot be directly perceived but are necessary for the consistency of a valid theory. A construct like C′, which is not connected with P and stretches only one rational arm to another C, is a hypothesized part of reality, waiting for a more complete incorporation into physical reality (for example, the neutrino, before it was experimentally discovered).

Within the C-field we have designated a region B. It is meant to represent the brain. This region belongs to the C-field and can be studied by the established methods of physical, chemical, and biological science.

Above P, in our symbolism, lies the mind. The different strata, designated thus far arbitrarily, are states or functions of the mind. Their vertical order represents what might be expressed as "distance from direct perception," awareness of things being the lowest (that is, the closest to P). The state in which the mind becomes aware of itself—self-consicousness or the ego—rises above the others; deliberate acts of the will, wherein the self exerts itself and incidentally interacts most strongly with the body, have been placed close to the self.

Now, as has already been indicated, there are no satisfactory known rules of correspondence (double-lined arrows) between the upper part of the figure and the lower. The dotted one marked R′ on the right, would represent a method for translating thoughts and feelings into measurable, and therefore quantifiable, constructs. Such methods, however, are extremely rudimentary ("just noticeable difference" methods), indirect (behaviorism), and loose (linguistic metaphors). Because of the failure of all attempts to translate mental states, mental observables that are subjectively clear, into quantitative constructs, we seem forced at this point to conclude that an explanation, a theory of the mind, is at present achievable in qualitative terms only.

Figures like 1 or 2 are drawn as finite diagrams. An extension at right angles to the plane of the drawing or in the plane adds nothing essential to the presentation, for it must be assumed that the P-plane is infinitely diverse, that new protocol experiences will be encountered as long as intellectual-sensory life exists. But an enlargement of this diagram up and down in the plane of the figure is suggestive. The C-field extending downward to infinity implies that theories tend to become infinitely detailed, which is indeed what present science and our epistemology entail.

But what is the meaning of allowing the upper, the mental, part of our diagram to extend to infinity? As drawn, the diagram represents the experiences of a single mind. Its states, which in the absence of a quantitative representation we can classify only in qualitative terms, may well be infinitely complex. This complexity can be indicated by an upward extension. Lateral extension suggests two things: (1) there are many minds, each of which constructs the same C-field if it proceeds along the lines our epistemology suggests. Beyond this observation we cannot legitimately go at present. Later, however, I shall have occasion to suggest and elaborate on the existence of a Universal Mind. I therefore list here suggestion (2): the lateral extension of the figure may mean a merging of all individual minds into a universal one.

I regard here another, possibly meaningful, suggestion that we owe to an anonymous member of an audience exposed to this epistemology. He suggested that figure 2 should be drawn on a cylinder of large dimension so that the upper and the lower edge of the figure coincide. This would mean that the mind would ultimately meet or merge with its own representation: the more remote the mental state, the more profound would be its interpretation. This suggestion has fascinating implications. It would mean that the deeper the mental state, the higher and more complex would be its scientific interpretation. Unusual constructs, constructs far removed from the P-plane, would correspond to or would be conceived in deepest intuition. Could this account for the inspiration of scientific genius which leads to bizarre conjectures that are ultimately verified empirically? Would it imply that the mind, in certain unusual states, could be aware of things that happen in the external world without reference to primary experience—in other words, clairvoyance?

Chapter 6

On the Meaning of Life, Mind, and Consciousness

Every statement that is to be meaningful to the scientist must contain words that have clearly defined meanings, except for a few singular terms that are either commonly understood or function as primitives, words not susceptible to and therefore not in need of definition. Words that are well understood are *cause* (determination of events by past conditions), *purpose* (determination of events by envisioned and intended future states), together with all empirically founded descriptive terms encountered in physics, chemistry, biology, and neurophysiology. Some crucial terms, with which this treatise abounds, however, are not clearly defined, nor is their meaning accessible through the type of analysis discussed in the preceding chapters. Chief among them are *life, mind, soul,* and *consciousness.*

Of these, I take *consciousness* as a *primitive.* For it is indefinable in terms of what we normally regard as empirical facts. Behavioristic attempts will hardly do as a general rule, for they presuppose an unexplained correspondence between aspects of consciousness and observable patterns of behavior. The choice of consciousness as primitive, on the other hand, is justified not only by the rules of logic but is made cogent by the fact that consciousness is at once the most immediate personal experience and the source from which all knowledge springs. I have previously emphasized that the external world is not "given" by outside agents but constructed from experiences of which we become or are immediately aware.

Awareness is part of consciousness; it refers to all experi-

ences we do not willfully engender, which assail us spontane-
ously. It is usually employed to designate the afferent aspects of
our consciousness. The common ones, listed by Eccles, are the
sensing of light, color, sound, smell, taste, pain, and touch.
These might be said to form "first order awareness": states in
which the sense of being a *self* is largely suppressed. Awareness
of being aware, or "second order awareness," also called self-
awareness or direct experience of the self, is a most intimate
aspect of consciousness. Intense concentration on it occurs but
rarely; a sense of self-awareness, however, accompanies all
mental acts or states. Only a trace of it is present in the sensing
process, in the feeling of my limbs or in reflex actions, while
most concentrated self-awareness accompanies whatever mental activity it induces in response to the question "Who am I?"

Between simple awareness, which contains responses to external stimuli, and concentrated, clear self-awareness, we experience a continuity of mixed or intermediate states.

The literature contains considerable discussion dealing with
the continuity of consciousness. Some writers, indeed, most
physiologists and medical experts, believe consciousness to be
interrupted by deep sleep, amnesia, and anesthesia. The evidence for this belief is not convincing. What is clearly true is
that the afferent, sensory activities are dimmed or suspended
and that in numerous instances the memory of what happened
during a certain interval is lost; but there is no proof that
self-awareness, the conscious ego, was interrupted: when the
patient awakes from the state of unconsciousness—perhaps a
somewhat misleading phrase—he knows that he is the same
person as the one who went to sleep. Furthermore, our self is
never aware of a continual change, the death and renewal of the
cells that make up our body and our brain. This fact has other
implications that will be dealt with later. At present I cite it as
evidence for the continuity of consciousness. To be sure, rec-
ords of split personalities and even altered personalities do
exist, but even in these instances there resides no proof that
existence of the central ego was ever changed or interrupted: it

may only acquire on occasion, or even permanently, different but less central attributes. I therefore feel, as did Schrödinger and other prominent writers, that the ego itself exists continuously throughout life.

But what is *life*? I cannot regard it as a primitive term without destroying the logic and validity of my arguments. Furthermore, the phenomenon of life belongs to the external world: our consciousness, our self, makes a judgment as to what objects in the world are alive. Now it is an amazing and perhaps amusing observation that the criteria defining life offered in textbooks on biology rarely agree. The ability to propagate and the ability to mutate, which ensure the survival and the evolutionary change of an object, called an organism if it possesses them, are the most common features employed to define life. Sinnott,[1] one of the great biologists who displayed creative insight as well as philosophic circumspection, was not content with these two defining characteristics. He added a third, the most important one in his opinion, and called it *organic form*, the "visible expression of an organized living system." To be more specific, Sinnott defined the spatial configuration of a living system as

> the result of growth correlations among its different parts and its various dimensions. The amount of growth in one direction or dimension is precisely related to that in others, and local differences in cellular character are so controlled that tissues and organs differentiate in a definite spatial order. The form of an animal or a plant is not a random association of parts, but a living whole.

To serve as a partial definition of life, the role I wish to assign to it, the last sentence should not contain the word "living"; let it therefore be excised.

I shall take as my empirical definition of life, or living things, a combination of the three criteria just mentioned: propagation, mutation, and organic form. Being descriptive, my definition can never satisfy the logician's demand of finality. Was an animal not alive when it lost the ability to procreate, or if it failed to undergo mutation? Schrödinger describes the material of a living protoplasm as an "aperiodic crystal," a physical object capable of having a characteristic form, of propagating, that is, growing in its own liquid, of taking a characteristic form, and (according to his view) mutating by means of alteration in its aperiodic structure. But we do not claim that it is alive. Biologists cite examples of entities in the shadowy regions between the living and the nonliving. There is speculation in some quarters that a robot may some day be constructed which complies with all three attributes of life I have cited. Will it be alive? In this context I remember two conversations with distinguished scientist-philosophers whose thoughts about these problems must have been deep because of their contributions. The first was Norbert Wiener, whom I asked: "Do you believe that ultimate mechanical refinement will ever make a computer conscious, or alive?" After some deliberation he replied: "No." The other was Philip Frank, the Harvard philosopher of science, who responded to the same question affirmatively. And to make his answer impressive and irrefutable he added: "You are an example!" Difficulties and contradictions of this sort always arise when an empirical definition of life is attempted. I shall therefore avoid it by returning to the one concept we know intuitively and at first hand, namely, consciousness. This we know directly within ourselves, and we impute it to other beings on grounds very similar to those that reveal external objects as real (see chapter 4), that is, they behave and react to circumstances as we do.

The scientific method that reifies certain of my sense impressions relies on rules of correspondence and contains metaphysical principles. On similar grounds, we recognize consciousness in others. Here we again use but reverse the rules of correspondence that led from our own sensations to the external objects. From the internal experience of seeing a color when I look in a certain direction, I infer the presence of that color within the context of impressions that lead to verification, to the postulation of an external object. Someone else looks in the same direction, evidently perceiving the same object. I then conclude that he too sees the red color. With human beings this conclusion can be confirmed by language or other forms of communication; but even aside from that, the conclusion is dictated by the principles of consistency, extensibility, and simplicity. This, by the way, is the only ground on which I can assert that the red you see is the same red as that experienced in my own consciousness.

This line of reasoning can be carried a little further. Other persons behave like myself in numerous respects; they seem to act with purpose and have bodies satisfying the three criteria of life mentioned above. They communicate with each other in many ways. All these facts, when subjected to the metaphysical principles mentioned, establish consciousness in others with the same certainty that accompanies our construction of real objects.

My final step is to *define* conscious creatures as being alive. The fact that many (if not all) of them also satisfy Sinnott's three empirical requirements adds cogency to this definition.

Retracing the logical steps by which we reached this conclusion, we say: Self-consciousness is a primitive, incapable of explicit definition. By the normal rules of correspondence and use of the normal metaphysical principles, we can recognize consciousness in others. Then follows the definition of life: All conscious things are alive.

This does not, of course, identify life with consciousness, for we have not determined whether all live creatures are conscious. Does life reside in things we deem inanimate? Is the entire universe alive, though partially unconscious? To these questions our present approach provides no answer: we can at this stage neither confirm nor reject panconsciousness, a belief prevalent in many eastern cultures. In short, we do not identify consciousness with life, but life is taken to be an attribute of consciousness. Whether there are living things that are not conscious is an unanswered question at this point in the discussion.

The manner in which, according to the preceding arguments, life is recognized as existing follows in every detail the rules of constructing physical reality. Elsewhere[2] I have called attention to alternate realities that play important roles in eastern thought and are apparently recognized as worthy of study in the West today. They are encountered in the state of meditation, in mystic experiences, hypnosis, even dreams. These are clear and well known, and they cannot be ignored in the study of the mind. An accepted epistemology, providing the rules of a passage from alternate realities to other nonphysical forms of reality does not exist, but may be emerging. Physical reality may be viewed as a set of constructs useful in the normal pursuit of life. But one can imagine, indeed experience, circumstances in which a different interpretation of conscious states has greater usefulness and greater explanatory power, in which a different kind of reality could or should be formulated.[3]

Thus, for instance, physical reality is not well suited to include feelings of sympathy, empathy, mutual understanding, friendship, and love. The universe of such emotions exists but is vague, unformulated, and finds expression in poetry, music, and other forms of art. This kind of reality, this universe, if more carefully established, might well provide better insignia of consciousness than the one I advocate here, the one based on and running parallel with physical reality. Empathy of one person for another, the feeling of mutual understanding, mystic union with another, or the "merging" of personalities yield in all probability different and perhaps better criteria of another person's consciousness than the one I have adopted. Mine, however, is sufficient for my purposes.

Now, one final thought. I shall endeavor to show, when discussing the arithmetical paradox, that two minds may be one even though the bodies are separate. This is no paradox if we accept as an alternate reality the world of shared feelings, of the *Weltgeist,* or of patriotism, for consciousness counted in one of the latter worlds is one, whereas bodies must be counted in the world of physical reality, where they are clearly many.

Thus far I have provided definitions for consciousness and for life, with a few digressions, to be sure. There remain the words *mind* and *soul*. The final step is simple. I take *mind* to be synonymous with consciousness and *soul* with self.

My approach to the central problems of psychology renounces an appeal to mechanistic physics. This is in contrast to much current literature, which is sometimes naive in its mechanistic implications. An example is a recent article in *Newsweek* entitled "A Baby's Need to Know."[4] The article informs the reader of the interesting fact that "the infant mind—thought to be a blank state at birth—is more complex than experts had ever imagined." Typical statements in the article include:

Scientists are learning about the mechanism of the human mind.

Babies quickly develop the notion of "self"—which suggests that the brain may be prewired for this concept.

[Habits of newborn babies] have apparently been prewired into the brain as firmly as the optic nerve.

Chapter 7
The Mind—Conjectures Based on Physics

In this brief survey I shall exclude innumerable attempts to explain consciousness or life in general by adding to already known physical agencies others bearing accustomed names but vague and unverified properties. Thus I forgo a discussion of a special postulated form of energy (called vital) and of vital force. It seems that we know enough about energy and forces to have discovered such special forms if they existed. I do not rule them out but regard their existence as unlikely. My earlier discussions also contain some evidence that psychic phenomena may not involve a transfer of energy or an exertion of force.

The hypotheses to be reviewed here are chiefly formulated by parapsychologists who wish to explain recent findings in their field, findings that are at odds with the materialistic theories of older psychologists and neurophysiologists. This is perhaps not surprising because the phenomenon of ordinary consciousness, which on critical examination contains extraordinary problems, has lost its fascination and its challenge and slumbers in the depths of behavioristic convictions. E. G. Boring[1] put it well when he said: "Psychology first lost its soul, then its mind, and then it lost its consciousness, but it still has behavior."

Earlier we arrived at the conclusion that the mind, whatever its physical or nonphysical nature, can perform a choice between physically open, statistically weighted alternatives. I used this thesis on earlier occasions[2] in seeking a solution to the philosophical problem of freedom of the will whose roots may even be found in Augustine's "De libero arbitrio." In the more recent literature the view that consciousness chooses among

quantum mechanical possibilities is found in the writings of
E. H. Walker[3] and N. Herbert,[4] who insist on a physical interpretation of mental processes and seek comfort and support in
some of the current controversies that enliven and confuse the
foundations of quantum mechanics. Some of their arguments,
notably those connecting simultaneous synaptic activation across
the entire brain with electronic tunneling, seem sound and
interesting, even though they do not throw light on the nature of
consciousness, which is here at issue. Three things, however, are
troublesome. One is their continual reference to what they call
the collapse of the state vector as a process connecting physics
with subjective knowledge of an observer. Another is their use of
obscure physical reasoning to make a case for consciousness as a
hidden variable. The third is their attempt to prove the occurrence of action at a distance. All of these bespeak the lack of
clarity even in the physicists' understanding of the bases of
quantum mechanics, and if that science is to be made the prime
vehicle into parapsychology the errors and inconsistencies encountered here must be exposed.

1. What is called the collapse of the state vector is an axiom
introduced by von Neumann and is correctly called the projection postulate. (The state vector does not collapse!) The axiom
states that when a measurement on a quantum system in state ψ
is performed and the result is the eigenvelue E_i, ψ is changed to
ψ_i, the eigenstate corresponding to E_i, so that if a similar measurement were performed immediately after the first the same
value E_i would be obtained. The term *collapse* is used in connection with a position measurement, where a wave packet ψ would
shrink—collapse—to a vertical line without width (a δ-function).

I have pointed out on several occasions[5] that (1) very few
actual measurements satisfy von Neumann's postulate; (2) it is
unnecessary: no empirically significant inferences are ever drawn
from it; and (3) the collapse of the wave packet contradicts other
established axioms of quantum mechanics. The omission of this
postulate leaves quantum mechanics viable and complete. We
shall therefore reject it.

2. The question as to the existence of "hidden variables," a term coined by Bohm, has been alive ever since the debate between Einstein and Bohr in 1927. Hidden variables are meant to satisfy the desire of many (in my view philosophically misguided) physicists to restore causality to quantum mechanics in the form of strict Laplacian determinism. I use the word "misguided" because it is becoming increasingly evident that every science is subject to epistemological feedback, a disturbance of being by the process of knowing (or measuring), and this ultimately leads to the use of probabilities as irreducible observables.

Hidden variables are supposedly hitherto unknown physical parameters whose insertion into physics will eliminate reference to probabilities. It seems to me that on a priori grounds hidden variables are unnecessary, indeed undesirable. In conformity with this conclusion Bell has been able to give a mathematically interesting and rather sweeping proof that hidden variables, in their normal sense, violate verified implications of quantum mechanics. Walker has seized on this result, asserting that if the hidden variables are not physical, they are mental. Unfortunately, this bare contention, true as it may be, leaves the nature of mind, which this essay is trying to explore, wholly enigmatic.

Consciousness is not a *variable* whose symbol could be put into Bell's inequality to render it untrue. In a previous, more disciplined study I equated "variable" with "observable," something that in principle can be quantified. Consciousness is a "system," an agent in my terminology, and it has many variables that may or may not be quantifiable in the physical sense. But to call it "hidden" involves a complete perversion of the facts of experience. All knowledge, including that of the physical world, starts with forms of awareness, usually sensations that, as explained previously, are transformed into the stable and coherent constructs that form the objects of the external world. Epistemologically, what is "hidden" at the beginning of every scientific process is the nature of the objects the process is designed to investigate. The sensations, the discoveries, the conjectures and hypotheses that prompt the investigation are "given," but given in consciousness. Their "existence" is indubitable, immediately evident—though what they imply (again via conscious processes) may be wrong. The word "hidden" is therefore utterly misleading, as is the noun "variable."

In fact, no philosopher has doubted the existence of consciousness prior to the query concerning hidden variables. To squeeze the existence of consciousness out of the crevasses of a physical theory is neither necessary nor useful.

Aside from all these difficulties the identification of consciousness with hidden variables throws no light on its intrinsic nature.

3. My third concern relates to the way in which Walker and Herbert and many others try to prove the possibility of action at a distance, which the theory of relativity is supposed to interdict. The inherent argument enjoys considerable support among current writers, so I will briefly summarize it here.

In 1935 Einstein, Podolski, and Rosen published a paper that led them to the conclusion that certain principles (among them the proposition that the transfer of information over a finite distance requires a finite time) were violated. The central idea was couched in a thought experiment: Two physical systems interact in close proximity, then separate in space. After a certain time each system is in a quantum state that permits, with assignable probabilities, statistically weighted outcomes of all possible measurements. A certain observable is measured on system 1, and this entails, according to the paper, a definite knowledge of what would have happened had a similar measurement been performed on system 2. The probabilities connected with the state of system 2 somehow congealed to certainties by virtue of an act on system 1. Hence there must have been an instantaneous communication between systems 1 and 2.

Physicists have the reputation of coining strange terms, a fact that sometimes irks the philosopher and the historian. They call the instantaneous transmission here occurring a "nonlocal effect" and speak of the problem of nonlocality. The good old term "action-at-a-distance," which has a lively and interesting history, would do as well.

Closer inspection of the Einstein et al. argument reveals that it is based in part on the projection postulate, which I have rejected.[6] I therefore disregard the nonlocality inference to which it is said to lead.

The preceding remarks were meant to be nothing more than a resolution of a current controversy; for my purposes it was a useless digression for there are other, wholly satisfactory grounds for believing in action at a distance in transmission of some characteristics of mental states at speeds greater than that of light. As we have seen, consciousness may not involve energy or matter, and we know of numerous physical phenomena, such as the phase velocity of light in a refractive medium (which carries no energy and cannot be used for signaling information), which travel with speeds exceeding c. One might also wonder what is meant by speed in connection with conscious awareness. If, on a starry night, I shift my gaze from one star to another, has anything traveled the distance between the two stars, which may be many millions of light years?

Let us again be reminded that consciousness, despite the desire of many physicists to adopt it, has not yet found a home in physics. We are reminded of the title of a most interesting book by the physicist Jean Charon:[7] *L'esprit, cet inconnu.* Charon makes a breathtaking suggestion. Consciousness, he proposes, is carried by the electrons within a living body, and the electrons are black holes! This thesis has much in its favor, for in a black hole the roles of space and time are interchanged; processes can go forward and backward in time; memory and even precognition are thus accounted for. But space, which within an electron is limited in any case, can be traversed in only one direction. A further attractive feature is this. The second law of thermodynamics requires that entropy within a closed system cannot decrease; order is normally destroyed. Only in living systems do order and information (negentropy) normally increase. A black hole is governed by the reverse of the second law: its entropy may decrease, its information may grow.

I see, however, a serious difficulty in this proposal. The condition for the existence of a black hole is

$$M/R \approx k(c^2/G)$$

where k is a constant of order of magnitude 1, M is its mass, R its radius, c the velocity of light, and G the constant of universal gravitation. If the values for M (the mass of an electron), c, and G are inserted, R turns out to be about 10^{-55} cm, which is exceedingly small in comparison with the electron's generally assumed radius of about 10^{-9} cm. To accept Charon's theory, a reason must be found for this discrepancy.

There is a good deal of parapsychological literature that, short of identifying the mind in physical terms, relies on physical *onta* to explain ESP and clairvoyance. An early, competent discussion of the way in which *tachyons* (*onta* with imaginary mass, first postulated by Terlietski) might serve to explain some mental phenomena was given by Adrian Dobbs (*Science and ESP*, ed. J. R. Smithies [Routledge and Kegan Paul, 1967]).

Some reliance on neutrinos may be found in Firsoff's *Life, Mind and Galaxies*.[8] A. Koestler, in his remarkable book *The Roots of Coincidence*,[9] also comments significantly on this possibility.

Satisfactory evidence for such conjectures, however, is not available at present, and if it were, these messengers of the mind would still leave its nature and its normal functions unexplained. One of the best sympathetic accounts of the compatability of parapsychology and physics has been given by Whiteman.[10]

In another recent book, *Future Science*,[11] several authors present views that rely in more oblique ways on physical conjectures. E. W. Russell revives the Burr-Northrop "theory of life," which relates the phenomenon of growth and, through somewhat risky extrapolation by other writers, life and consciousness to the action of electrostatic fields. The facts given by Burr and

Northrop are not under dispute, but it is difficult to find an explanatory use of this hypothesis for the various aspects of consciousness.

V. M. Inyushin[12] accounts for life, and thus presumably for consciousness, by postulating a fifth state of matter (in addition to solid, liquid, gaseous, and plasma states). A living organism is said to be characterized by a "biofield," a physical entity. The biofield has a definite physical shape, at times an auralike projection beyond the body, and even an extensive spread over distances that might account for telepathy. As to its nature, it is purely physical, consisting of ions, free electrons, and free protons. The paper reports experimental investigations supposed to deal with this novel fluid, which is said to be normally attached to the brain. Physicists are not likely to be convinced of the biofield's existence as a *new* form of matter and energy. Ions, electrons, and protons are surely present within the cells of the brain, but they can hardly be conceived as performing the tasks that a conscious mind has to accomplish.

In the same book[13] G. Wachsmut exploits the extravagant hypothesis that there are four different kinds of ether, using a theory proposed by the anthroposophist Rudolf Steiner. Wachsmut's claims are entirely at variance with present physical theory and do not illuminate the mysteries of the mind, nor are they necessary to support Steiner's views.

H. C. Dudley[14] also presents reasons designed to convince the physicist of the existence of an ether, this time a single one, conceived as a sea of neutrinos. The physical reasons Dudley gives are interesting even though they contradict what is now commonly accepted. But the relevance of a neutrino ether to mind is obscure and hardly touched on, except in a couple of sentences suggesting that neutrinos might be called on for the transmission of information. At any rate, neutrinos are subject to experimentation that has thus far not revealed the neutrino's importance to parapsychology or to the functions of the mind.

E. H. Walker and N. Herbert[15] proclaim consciousness to be a hidden variable in a sense introduced by Bohr. Much of what is said in this paper makes contemporary sense and follows arguments I have already discussed and criticized in the earlier parts of this chapter. I feel, as already indicated, that the term "hidden" is completely misleading. It would indeed be more appropriate to apply the term "hidden variables" to the features of the external world, the scientific constructs, for they are inferred from states of consciousness, which are primary, immediate, and open to the self, and it is their rationalization, their interpretation, that leads to our understanding of the external world and to the "ordinary" physical variables—some of which may still be hidden.

C. Muses[16] believes that "empty space" is the obvious candidate for the prime transducer or mediator between matter and consciousness. His paper, unfortunately, does not present sufficient grounds for this assumption; it merely hints at his theory of "hyper numbers" as providing evidence for empty spaces. Muses does, however, address the problem of consciousness squarely, not obliquely via parapsychology, and ends with an avowal of panconsciousness, a view I shall be led to consider seriously later in this book.

Chapter 8
The Mind Viewed as a Field

To sum up the foregoing chapter: present day physics seems to contain no agency directly identifiable with the mind. It has renounced the philosophy of materialism that dominated its earlier phases, replacing it by more elusive doctrines which offer a wider range of explanation. One of the general concepts that has received increasing emphasis, wider application and greater refinement is that of a field. Hence it may be appropriate to devote this chapter to a simple, though general discussion of it.

Many of the important nonmaterial entities of modern physics are called *fields*. Most of these, while not themselves material, are closely associated with and descriptive of the properties of matter. Examples already cited include the flow field of a moving fluid, the electric and magnetic fields surrounding bodies, the temperature field of the atmosphere, and the stress field within a compressed solid. None of these, however, is strictly speaking material, even though all are meaningful only in the presence of matter. Indeed, the concept of field has taken on a measure of importance and independence that rivals, and perhaps overshadows, that of matter in recent physics.

Then there are numerous fields that are not attached to matter and could never be called material. I refer here to gravitational force fields, to the metric field in general relativity, to radiation fields, to several abstract fields occurring in nuclear physics which are still under investigation. These can be described by such esoteric, not to say esthetic qualities as invariance, symmetry, etc. One of the most distinguished living physicists, Dirac, even discusses them in terms of the beauty of the mathematical equations that express their properties. Above all, and in addition to these, there are the probability fields encountered among the basic observables of quantum mechanics. The state function *phi,* whose square designates a probability, was briefly discussed in chapter 3. Most of the laws descriptive of the microcosm contain it, and it forms a nonmaterial field; the function[1] $\varphi(x)$ referring to a point of space denoted by the argument does not imply that any matter exists at x.

The term *probability field* may be a novelty to many readers. Since it characterizes the quintessence of quantum mechanics and introduces a face of reality wholly different from its predecessors in classical physics I explain it in terms of a simple metaphor, with apologies to the mathematical reader.

Imagine you aim a rifle at a target. Even if you are an excellent marksman the chances of your hitting the bull's eye are not 100 percent. For there are innumerable disturbances: there is a physiologically inevitable, perhaps not noticeable vibration of your body and your arm; there are air currents affecting the path of the bullet; there are small fluctuations in the position of the target because the ground on which it stands is subject to tremors—none of these disturbances can be controlled effectively. And if the bull's eye is a point you will surely miss it. There is, however, a finite possibility that your bullet will strike a certain specifiable area near the target center. What does this mean?

Suppose you divide the area of the target into segments. For simplicity, let the boundaries of the segments be concentric circles around the bull's eye and label the concentric circular segments by numbers: 1 for the innermost circle, 2 for the one next surrounding it, 3 for the next, and so on. You now shoot at the target 100 times, always aiming at the bull's eye, and then you record and analyze the impacts. For simplicity, let us assume that area 1 contains 20 impacts, area 2 contains 15, area 3 contains 10, area 4 receives 5, and all the rest of the target area contains 50. By probability the mathematician means the number of impacts in a given area divided by the total number of shots: thus the probability of hitting area 1 is 0.10, that of area 2 is 0.15, and so forth. The probability of striking the area outside of the fourth circle is .50, or one half. This assignment of probabilities to the different areas is called a probability distribution or, if it refers to spatial domains, a probability field. It is clearly a measure of the "chance" that a given shot will hit the domain (the area or the space) to which the probability refers. Knowing the probability field, only the relative frequency of impacts at different places can be predicted; what happens in a given shot remains unknown.

The marksman has the power, however, to change the probability distribution, the field. He can do this in two ways: by changing his aim and by changing his distance from the target. He can even cause the entire probability field to collapse, to become merely a point or a small area around the bull's eye, by bringing his gun right up to the target. The inner area then has a probability of 1 to be struck, all others have a probability of zero. We then say the probabilities have condensed or congealed to certainty. Anticipating matters to be discussed next I shall speak of the procedures that produce different probability fields as "preparations" of the state of the bullets.

I now turn to quantum mechanics to discuss what happens when an electron is shot from an electron gun at a target, where its impact is observed as a scintillation. Everything said about the bullet remains true for the electron; the target is the locus of a probability field describing the frequency of impacts of an electron or, what amounts in the case to the same thing, the fraction of electrons in a swarm hitting a given area. Again, preparation of the state of the electrons is possible to produce different fields.

The field in this instance as in the case of the bullet is defined on a plane; it is two-dimensional. If the screen were moved to another place near the target, however, it would also be struck by electrons, but with different frequencies, that is, with different probabilities. In principle, therefore, every small volume tranversed by electrons has its own probability to be struck: the probability field is 3-dimensional.

So far our two accounts concerning the behavior of bullets and electrons have been very similar. In both instances state preparation produces a probability field that will in general be different for different kinds of preparation. But if we go beyond description of what happens and look for reasons or causes of the projectiles' behavior, for causes of the probability fields, an enormous contrast appears.

The behavior of the bullets can be satisfactorily explained by classical prequantum physics, which looks for external agencies, like the disturbances mentioned earlier, to account for the departure of the bullet from its preset goal, that is, to explain the need for probabilities. Classical physics holds that if these perturbations are known exactly and included in the calculation of the bullet's path the precise point of impact can be predicted on the basis of mechanical, strictly causal laws. The need for using probabilities is therefore to be seen in the difficulty, nay, practical impossibility, of including all effects in the theory. A highly refined and complicated computer could in principle eliminate this need. And there is a wealth of traditional evidence to substantiate this view in the molar world. Hence probabilities and probability fields are secondary, derivative kinds of entities that occur in the science of mechanics *à faute de mieux*.

For electrons the story is entirely different. There exists at present no theory that could possibly succeed in eliminating the use of probabilities in the experiment described. All we can do is calculate the probabilities, not the electron paths. In fact quantum mechanics, the theory here applicable, does not contain the idea of a path; indeed it usually leads to contradictions if a path is assumed. Probabilities are the ultimate concepts in the theory of electron behavior. And nothing else is needed to make the theory complete.

This result has profound philosophical implications. In classical mechanics the notion of path is tolerated and indeed needed for analyzing the behavior of molar bodies. This fact implies to the philosopher of science that body and path exist, that they are real. The probability field is compatible with the existence of paths and therefore also real, but only in a sort of derivative, secondary sense. In quantum theory, where there is no path, probabilities take on the character of primary, of ultimate concepts or observables. They cannot be washed away by deeper theories or more refined observations, at least for now. And the theory is beautiful in structure and complete. Probability fields therefore take the place of paths, and if the latter were regarded as real in classical mechanics the former deserve the attribute of reality in the domain ruled by quantum theory. Hence my concern in this book is with probability fields that are abstract, immaterial, quite different in essence from electromagnetic and other kinds of field. Yet, as the reader will realize on closer thought, they satisfy all requirements we have placed on physical observables.

In concluding this discussion one might wonder whether, since probabilities seem ultimate in the microworld of electrons (et al.), a union of classical and quantum mechanics cannot be brought about by reversing the customary approach and affirming that even in ordinary mechanics we are ultimately dealing with probabilities that, however, are unimportant in the macroworld or the molar realm. This would imply that absolutely certain knowledge is never at hand where empirical observations are concerned. Einstein's dictum "God does not play dice" might still be true; but it is man's fate to encounter uncertainties inevitably in all his observations. I do not feel that this is an unreasonable epistemological premise, for every measurement is subject to an uncertainty dealt with in the mathematical theory of errors. Even the most refined measurements of physical constants, which may be reported in a dozen significant figures, are always followed by ± a second number, usually one or two figures, which denotes the probable error, the uncertainty in its value.

Hence the assumption of the inevitability of probabilities and probability fields in all of science, in all of human empirical knowledge, their universal reality, is an attractive but debatable philosophic view.

I now return to quantum mechanics.

The reader who is inclined to regard a probability field, like φ, as merely an auxiliary artifact relating ultimately to something material should be reminded of the following: Probabilities are proper, indeed irreducible, observables satisfying the same methodological requirements as do such quantities as position, velocity, energy, or mass. The reasons for this claim were discussed in chapter 4 where it is shown that every observable acceptable to science must meet two criteria: first, it must be linked to perceptible experience (P-plane) by some rule of correspondence, usually a Bridgmannian operational definition, and second, it must be lodged within a consistent complex of theoretical constructs (C-field) that ensure its predictive usefulness. Probabilities satisfy both requirements. They have only one apparently unique and peculiar idiosyncrasy: their rule of correspondence stipulates not a single but a multitude of observations. This, however, does not invalidate their use as proper observables in science nor their valid role as constituents of physical and perhaps other types of reality.

We might further amplify these remarks by recalling that the social sciences, too, cast probabilities in important roles. The ultimate "observable" on which the life insurance actuary depends in his reckoning is the death rate within a population, that is, the probability that a given person will die; the economist projects probabilities, not materialistic certainties, on the basis of numerous observations called statistics. Finally, when a situation is fully analyzed, even the classical, old-style physicist must admit that a single observation or measurement rarely satisfies his desire for precision. To obtain the "true" value of the quantity, the scientist must make many observations and apply the theory of errors, of probability, in ascertaining the value he considers to be true. I conclude that all through science probability fields are as important, necessary, and real as any other construct of science. They are true and valid observables.

Among the many fields mentioned here, φ is most likely to be among those that baffled the old-style materialist. Needless to say, φ may have reference to photons and to other massless *onta*.

If there is a mind that is not an effluvium of the body or an epiphenomenon coming into play at a certain stage of organization of matter, we face the question "Is it only controlled by the body or can it also control the body?" I answered this query affirmatively in chapter 3.

From what has been said it appears that the concept of mind or consciousness resembles most closely what physicists call a field; it is not necessarily localized in a limited region but is capable of being located predominantly within a given space, say, a human body. This is perhaps one's first conjecture. The adequacy of this concept, however, cannot be taken for granted; for even in physics we have encountered *onta* that have only latent positions or locations. Although science no longer forces us to regard mind as material, or even as associated with matter, we do know that it interacts with matter, primarily the brain.

I will briefly restate some of my earlier conclusions in this context. Most modern biologists, even those who grant a measure of independence to the mind, still hold the view that everything mental is somehow "caused" by processes within the brain. These biologists tend to deny reciprocal action. We find absolutely no evidence for this asymmetric belief that is unsatisfactory even on logical or metaphysical grounds. Its inadequacy appears even more clearly in the recent neurophysiological discoveries mentioned at the end of chapter 3. In an earlier book[2] LeShan and I discussed the freedom of the will. Here, I merely note that every person feels instinctively that his mind can direct his bodily movements, and this instinctive awareness is as clear and basic as any sensory impression, such as my seeing an external object. There are, of course, hallucinations.

These are exposed as unreal (in the physical sense) on two grounds: (1) they cannot be verified by other persons (empirical confirmation), and (2) there is no otherwise valid theory that allows them to be referred to as external objects. (Cf. Metaphysical Principles) As *mental* phenomena, they are being explained by psychologists.

Now, the thesis that our mind controls our bodily movements clearly contradicts statement 1, for every person is continually aware of the mind's control of the body and confirms this for others. Statement 2, to the contrary, is unfortunately true, but only because we do not possess a generally acceptable theory of the mind. The search for one has inspired the present considerations. As an empirical fact, however, I shall henceforth take for granted the possibility or, better, the general occurrence of a reciprocal action between body and mind.

This raises the question as to the nature of the interaction between the immaterial mind and the material body. Interaction between immaterial and material *onta* are known to occur, indeed abound, in modern physics and engineering. Every electric motor depends on it. Now in most of these there is an exchange of energy, and the first hypothesis that presents itself is that a similar exchange takes place between mind and body. To maintain this view we shall have to postulate some form of mental energy. This is a common approach to the mind-body interaction problem, favored by many parapsychologists. But we do not need to commit ourselves to this view at this stage, because there exists at present no cogent definition of mental energy, at least the physicist knows of none. Further evidence may someday justify the construct mental energy, which at present has only metaphoric meaning.

Let us then at this point ask the question "Are all interactions occurring in the physical world of the nature of energy exchanges, and is energy always conserved?" The answer to the first part of the question is negative, for there are control or guidance mechanisms in which no work is done and hence no energy is transferred. A typical example is a train going around a curve. Here the rails press against the wheels of the car, thus exerting a force. But the force is at right angles to the displacement; hence no work is done. It is easy to cite many similar examples.

As for energy conservation, it is more difficult to find examples of its failure, certainly none in the macrocosm. In quantum mechanics, however, some do occur. Earlier I mentioned the barrier problem in which a charged particle can traverse a barrier that it has insufficient energy to surmount. To account for this classically forbidden phenomenon, the physicist ascribes "negative kinetic energy," a term that is intrinsically meaningless, to the particle while it is inside the barrier. The effect of the barrier is to reduce the number of particles passing through but not their energy. Again, it changes a probability field.

In some instances, notably in the process of scattering, where an atomic or molecular system makes a transition from one energy state to another, calculation shows that the system can pass through intermediate states of energy greater than the initial and final one. To relieve the strangeness of this process, physicists mask its essence by calling the intermediate states "virtual," presumably as distinct from real. But even if these states are never final and permanent, it is hard to see that they are not real if they are needed to explain what happens. Finally, we call attention once more to the interconvertability of energy and mass, which implies, of course, that energy can appear or disappear, the gain or loss being in terms of mass.

In conclusion, then, one may say that conservation of energy is still a generally valid principle in practically all of known science but that it is being nibbled at by a few fringe phenomena discovered only in this century. I therefore prefer, for the present at least, not to abandon the principle when discussing the interaction of mind and body. This is not to preclude the issue, for science is an ever advancing discipline for which ultimate truth is at best an asymptotic concept, an ideal toward which science slowly advances and which may never be in its finite grasp. There are doubtless forms of energy of which we are completely unaware—among them possibly mental energy, but it is my strategy here to see how far one can go with the use of currently accepted scientific tools. And that distance is considerable.

We have seen that in quantum mechanics, so-called classical observables can be latent. For a given φ, numerous values of a quantity like position, velocity, or spin of an *on* may emerge when a measurement is made or, to put it differently now, when it interacts with another system. All these values, each carrying a definite probability, are equivalent as far as the other system is concerned; whichever occurs, that system has no choice in the matter. Neither does it have to supply energy to bring the interaction about. In some instances the measuring apparatus will receive or supply energy, but such a transfer is "voluntary," automatic, adjusted to whatever value of the observable appears. For our purposes, however, we can ignore these cases: we may regard the measuring agent as a pure spectator who merely tells the value of the observable as it turns up.

In very complicated physical systems such as the brain, the neurons, and sense organs, whose constituents are small enough to be governed by probabilistic quantum laws, the physical organ is always poised for a multitude of possible changes, each with a definite probability; if one change takes place that requires energy, or more or less energy than another, the intricate organism furnishes it automatically. Hence, even if the mind has anything to do with the change, that is, if there is mind-body interaction, the mind would not be called on to furnish energy.

Finally, I mention in this context another quantum mechanical situation that bears on the conservation problem. A microsystem may be in a state φ in which the energy itself is latent. Such states are called *nonstationary,* and φ would be a function of space coordinates as well as time. In that case different measurements, interactions with outside apparatus (including sense organs) would yield different energies at different times, again regulated by probabilities. Here the system itself clearly does not conserve energy from instance to instance. On closer analysis, however, this case is similar to the one discussed in the previous paragraph; for there is usually a medium adjacent to or engulfing the system in a nonstationary state (such as a radiation field) which pays the energy bill.

The conclusion to which the considerations of this chapter have led us may be summarized as follows. The mind may be regarded as a field in the accepted physical sense of the term. But it is a nonmaterial field; its closest analogue is perhaps a probability field. It cannot be compared with the simpler non-material fields that require the presence of matter (for example, hydrodynamic flow field or acoustic fields). Nor does it neces-sarily have a definite position in space.[3] And so far as present evidence goes it is not an energy field in any physical sense, nor is it required to contain energy in order to account for all known phenomena in which mind interacts with brain.

I add one final thought. In physics the more massive an object the more satisfactorily can its behavior be represented by materialistic methods. The uncertainty principle ensures that the lighter an *on*, the less definite becomes its position, its velocity, and other material quantities, the more it resembles a field (electron) or becomes itself a field (photon). The mind has no mass at all. Hence it is not surprising that it partakes of the properties of a field: immateriality, lack of position, or even spatial confinement; these are unusual and abstract features that require novel methods of investigation.

Chapter 9

Science and Religion

Preceding chapters presented evidence for viewing the external world as a product of the mind, constructed under definite, universal rules. This conclusion does not, of course, prevent us from making a basic distinction between external world and mind, and it also permits us with certain reservations to speak of the external world in a conventional sense.

Later parts of this book approach the realm of religion, a subject that seeks in numerous ways and with a great variety of results to harmonize knowledge of the external world with the more intricate concerns of the mind. I therefore think it desirable to insert here a brief chapter relating our knowledge of the world to some aspects of religion.

Chapter 4 dealt in some detail with the method and the epistemology by which the reality of the external world is established. I called it the method of science, more particularly, the method of physical science.

My thesis was that primary (P) experiences, the edge of the C-field, are subjective, contingent, qualitative, and by themselves incoherent; they form part of what Kant called the "rhapsody of perceptions." Because of the lack of rational relations among them, P-facts require to be organized, made stable, "objective," rationally tractable, by translation into constructs via rules of correspondence.

One of the essential ingredients of most religions is a belief in the existence of God, or gods, residing in some sort of heaven, and perhaps other nonscientific entities. Hence it is useful at this point to give thought to the meaning of *existence in different domains*. To the materialist the answer is simple and need not be reviewed. It has practically no relevance for religion. But I have indicated in this book and elsewhere that physicists have been forced to tolerate a more abstract view of existence. To be sure, they still identify existence with reality, and the method of establishing reality has been discussed.

Perhaps it is clear from our earlier examples that existence, even in science, is not a simple thing to comprehend or to demonstrate. The meaning of statements alleging existence, validity, and truth may be very far from anything that common sense conveys. Such assertions will occupy our attention once more in the following chapter.

There is a view, held by some advocates of religion, claiming that our definition of reality has no relevance for their cherished doctrine, that religious experience arises not from the methods I have described but from an approach via *intuition*. What this means and how it works has been discussed at some length in an earlier publication[1] and need not be repeated here. My conclusion is that a form of intuition, divine inspiration that proves true in an empirical sense or useful in providing ethical rules for human action, may form an important example for a certain type of intuition.

Central to the tenets of every religion is the interaction between God and man. Here, I believe, one encounters two essential problems: first, the nature of God's intervention in human lives, and second, the renowned problem of evil, which poses difficulties in view of God's omniscience, omnipotence, and all-goodness, attributes most religions maintain even though they seem incompatible.

Turning to the problem of intervention, I bring forth two distinguishable views. One, most commonly accepted by scientists, holds that intervention occurs through natural events that happen at appropriate times within a human life. Examples are a seemingly miraculous escape from an accident, the unexpected cure of an illness, painless death after a terminal disease, the answer to a prayer, or the emergence of a sudden insight (intuition in senses *a* or *b* of note 1), even in scholarly research. All these instances tolerate both a scientific and a religious interpretation.

Less specific, and more common among formalized religions, is a solution of the intervention problem that identifies intervention with past events, events revealing "divine providence." This aspect was thoroughly and extensively treated by the distinguished physicist-theologian William G. Pollard in his book *Chance and Providence, God's Action in a World Governed by Scientific Thought.*[2] Pollard's analysis is based on the Judeo-Christian theologies but permits extension to several other religions. He leads the reader to his theme by first making two distinctions: one separates physical from historical reality,[3] the other scientific from historic time.[4] Scientific time, which characterizes scientific reality, is an abstract idea employed in the description of observable processes. It is represented by a line in space and has an arbitrary origin denoting the present, but the present has no absolute significance and can be located by choice anywhere on the line. The left of its origin designates an arbitrary past, the right an indefinite but expected future. But historical time "has no extension and cannot be measured. It can only be lived. It is made up of three domains—past, present and future—each of which is different and possesses its own distinctive future." Historical reality differs from scientific reality in the absolute inability of the historian to experiment with its events. He can never confirm his hypotheses or his laws by discovering what would have happened if other historical facts had prevailed. Thus Pollard asserts that "chance, and through chance providence, are irrefutably parts of historical reality and events in historic time." Pollard uses as an example the exodus of the Jews from Egypt (in an early version), Yahweh's driving back the sea to let the Jews pass, then returning the waters to drown the pursuing Egyptians. Pollard rejects the idea of Providence as an added nonphysical force in nature "whose operation produces discernable and verifiable empirical consequences by means of which it can be objectively established." Incidents like the exodus derive their validity as occurrences of providence from the religious awe with which they were reported.

I now turn to our second theme, which relates to the interaction between God and man, a theme that culminates in the problem of evil. If God is almighty, all-knowing, and all-good, how could he tolerate evil in his world?

One answer simply denies the premise, which assumes that there is also a mighty devil who endeavors to capture human souls. Primitive religions accept this premise in various forms, but most modern creeds view the assumption as superstition. Or else they place an evil disposition in man himself, assuming him to be responsible for his choice of action. This vesting of responsibility in man, however, deprives God of his omnipotence. A slight modification of this version interprets God's goodness as allowing man a certain freedom with which God does not interfere. He deliberately relinquishes part of his power but imposes justice, that is, punishment.

Then there is the radical but also trivial solution of Somerset Maugham,[5] presented as an allegory involving an encounter in heaven. Three people, a man and two women, who on earth were involved in a love triangle, appear at the gate of heaven awaiting their fate. John had been married for five years to Mary when he fell in love with Ruth. He nevertheless remained faithful to Mary, even though he hated her. Ruth maintained her innocence but lived unhappily. Now they stood as ghosts in pallor awaiting the Lord's judgment.

There was also a philosopher, ready to receive his fate. He had addressed the Eternal: "No one can deny the fact of Evil. Now if God cannot prevent Evil he is not all-powerful, and if he can prevent it he is not all-good." And furthermore: "I will not believe in a God who is not All-Powerful and All-Good." The end of the story is this: The Eternal blew lightly, "as a man might blow out a lighted match, and behold! where there were three poor souls—was nothing." Then he turned to the philosopher saying: "You cannot but allow that on this occasion I have

very happily combined my All-Power with my All-Goodness."
He was good enough to annihilate them in compensation for
their previous suffering, of which he knew because of his
omniscience.

The story, while making a point, is not likely to impress the
philosopher, for it contains a bit of cynicism its author probably intended.

The other solution to the problem of evil, the one I prefer,
is simply this. Suffering is mistaken for evil. If man were
omniscient he might regard it as good in the full context of all
events, past, present, and future, psychic as well as physical.
This view, the reader will see, is also most compatible with the
conclusions of the final chapter of this book where it will be
restated more explicitly.

And the last consideration, compatible with the preceding,
is this. God created not only the world but also the laws of
nature, to which he agreed to adhere.[6] Everything that happens, including evil events, is in accord with these laws and
therefore in the strictest sense necessary. The strange conclusion is therefore that absence of what man regards as evil
would be a miracle.

In one of my essays in *Religious Doctrine and Natural
Science, Physics, and Philosophy* I also discuss how new aspects of science have lessened the strain on religion and why
arguments based on "common sense" are no longer adequate
to invalidate all religious doctrines. Further, I discuss the view
that religion may be a "metascience," a discipline with its own
structure, which ponders the somewhat miraculous circumstance that man is able to apply the scientific method and that
the unruly mass of factual (P) experiences can be made to
obey simple rules and laws. Considering the contrast between
the striking simplicity and elegance of the constructional
scheme on the one hand and the formidable welter of contin-
gencies of the primary facts on the other, man succumbs to a
feeling of surprise, as though he confronted a miracle. The
theologian Sohleiermacher phrased this sentiment—the mir-

acle of natural order—with unforgettable eloquence in his speeches to the German nation. If this sentiment be religious, science does indeed engender it.

The essay goes on to examine the view that religion may be regarded as an enlargement of experience in the "existential" domain. Reference is made to the views of Heidegger, Kierkegaard, Gabriel Marcel, and Sartre.

Finally, I raise the question whether religion could be part of an enlarged science, whether it can have its own primary experience (a kind of P-plane) from which religious inferences can be drawn. There are experiences that are often regarded as distinct sources of religious beliefs. Examples are the awe in the presence of overwhelming beauty, the feeling of gratitude for human existence, the contrition that follows a sinful act, the feeling of misery and abandon at our impatience before fate, our longing for grace and redemption, the mystical communion with the infinite which the saints describe as an encounter with God, our frightened exposure to the "tremendum," and finally our despair at the prospect of irrevocable annihilation. Yet to say that these are peculiarly religious experiences is not to argue that they are *exclusively* religious. For they are also P-facts for several of the psychological and social sciences. This, however, does not cast out the possibility of an analysis in religious terms, nor does it show such experiences to be irrelevant or illegitimate. For a simple sensation may well be the starting point of several inquiries, one into a physical, the others into a biological or a psychological domain of constructs. This fact must always be recognized and is no argument against the validity of any of the explanatory schemes.[7] And, in this context, religion also can claim its due.

If religion is to have the structure of science, it must also expose itself to tests in the manner of our circuits of empirical verification. This requirement forces us to reject at once certain peculiar kinds of theology, such as the deism of the Enlightenment and probably also predetermination of the Calvinistic type. For these theories could never be tested, not even in the

mild sense of Pollard's Providence. Any tests man could devise
would be foreordained, would have been included in the Creator's foresight at the very beginning. It would, therefore, be
futile to regard the outcome of the tests as significant. But such
criticisms do not affect most major theological systems.

Finally, there are some points of contact between modern
science and traditional religion. I will cite a few instances
demonstrating approaches between some fairly universal religious tenets and modern science in concluding this chapter. An
act of creation is a typical ingredient of many religious beliefs.
Old-style science denied this by an appeal to certain conservation principles (matter, energy). Thomas Aquinas's *creatio ex
nihilo* was regarded as absurd,[8] but it has now been shown that a
sphere of matter having sufficient density, and thus possessing
positive mass energy (mc^2) and negative potential energy because of gravitational attraction, may have a zero total energy
as well as zero momentum. Hence it would satisfy all known
conservation laws if it were created out of nothing. The big
bang theory does not contradict this conjecture (see chapter 8).

Science and religion touch each other on a very basic plane in
the biblical account of the Flood, for in its aftermath Jehovah
grants as it were a charter to science, with an implication that
the two shall live in peace. Reference is here not to the first act
of creation in Genesis I, which resulted in the existence of a
physical universe, but to a second, equally important one,
which established the lawfulness of the universe. First, we are
told, there was chaos, *tohu vavohu*; a period of this lawlessness
and confusion was termined by the Flood.

One interpretation of the turbulent days prior to the Flood
which is elaborated in the Jewish Talmud emphasizes that
during this period nature, and nature's God, did not act in
accordance with causal principles, that there were no natural
laws and hence no possibility for natural science. Lawfulness,
behavior in conformity with reasonable principles, and causality
were God's gift to Noah, made in the beautiful covenant of the
rainbow.

Some of the miracles reported in the Bible become acceptable as instances of psychic healing. Other points of contact, especially with eastern religions, will appear in the last chapter.

At this point, I venture to include a somewhat irrelevant comment on a prevalent popular view which holds that most scientists are somehow antireligious. Statistics (of which I am not aware!) might well bear this out. But it is my distinct impression that truly creative scientists, especially those of our era whom I have had the privilege to know, belie this popular belief.

This chapter has dealt briefly with the relation between generally accepted sciences and religion. Elsewhere[9] I have endeavored to show that ethics, too, has a structure similar to science. In most religions ethics is more closely related to religion than are the sciences, for ethics forms either the beginning or the end point of many theologies. Divine inspiration often provides the commandments, the beginnings of an ethical system; divine reward or punishment forms the end.

Chapter 10

A Universal Mind?

Examination of the earliest recorded religions reveals three common features: polytheism, animism, and at slightly later stages a strangely enduring doctrine, the belief in some form of Universal Mind accessible to the individual under suitable circumstances. A great variety of names have described this Universal Mind, among them Tao, Logos, Brahman, Atman, the Absolute, Mana, Holy Ghost, Weltgeist, or simply God.[1] Belief in this concept is especially pronounced in eastern cultures. In this chapter I wish to analyze this idea in more or less western and modern terms.

The postulation of a Universal Mind, of which each conscious being and perhaps every entity composing the world is a part, creates obvious difficulties, primarily for the western scientist. For it seems perfectly clear that my thoughts and feelings are different from everybody else's, and that they cannot be identified. The problem we face here would clearly not even arise for the materialist or mechanist, who discovered that the brain states of different individuals are different, a fact that to him is convincing evidence for the thesis that no two minds can be the same. These two points—*indirect* (not immediate!) knowledge of the difference of mental states in different persons and the mechanist's empirical findings regarding brain states—block the road to the conception of a single, Universal Mind.

The absence of a science of consciousness, which we emphasized in an earlier book[2] and in preceding chapters, indeed our objective ignorance of the very nature of consciousness, make it difficult, perhaps impossible to refute the mechanist's arguments. But if these arguments are taken to be true, all the difficulties we have noted in connection with the identity theory of mind and brain and of the epiphenomenal view of mind return to plague us. Hence the attempt I make here to establish the oneness of minds, even if it is feeble and certain to be rejected by the mechanist, is nevertheless worthwhile and perhaps of crucial importance.

Before approaching this idea, and in hopes of making it less repulsive to the modern physicist, I recall a feature of recent nuclear theory, a feature embedded in a current gauge theory of *onta*. This theory does not suggest that different *onta* merge into one, but it takes a step toward such a view by claiming that *onta* lose their identity, though not their number.

Two instances come to mind. The first relates to protons and neutrons. When these are separated in space and therefore not interacting, one is charged and the other is neutral. But at sufficiently close distances their identities disappear, their properties merge, and a distinction between them becomes impossible. But they are still two *onta*.

Scientists now assume three different fundamental forces between the constituents of the nuclear world. The strength of these forces, however, depends on the energy of the interacting entities. It differs enormously between the three at small energies of interaction. Strangely, however, the three forces approach equal values at extremely high energies if current theories are correct. There are empirical indications of this tendency, but the state of equality has not yet been reached experimentally.

A loss of identity that would have been incomprehensible to scientists only a few decades ago has now become acceptable. In view of this, perhaps the following comments will seem less strange.

My first point concerns the meaning of the phrase "to be part of." It may give the mechanist an unexpected blow. I shall present a personal experience that seems relevant to this inquiry. In a 1940 paper entitled "Reality in Quantum Mechanics," I introduced the idea of the "latent observable,"[3] a concept similar to one invoked by Heisenberg in his later writings under the Aristotelian name potency or potentiality. The reasoning is this.

The state of a quantum system cannot be described in terms of the ordinary observables of classical mechanics and all other sciences dealing with large scale physical phenomena. An atomic particle, an *on,* is usually in a state the knowledge of which allows only the assignment of probabilities to the value of an "ordinary" variable, such as energy, momentum, or position of, say, an electron. Many values compose the same state, characterize the same entity. But when a measurement is made, a definite value of the variable appears. Orthodox theory, prevalent at the time, held that prior to the measurement, the electron *was* in a definite classical state, having, let us say, a definite momentum but a value unknown to the observer. The measurement revealed a value to the observer,[4] and after the measurement the electron continued to move on with the thus exposed, observed momentum value. This theory runs into numerous difficulties (see note 3) that led to the proposal of the latency theory.

According to this theory, the electron, in its premeasurement state, did not necessarily "have" or "possess" a definite momentum. The momentum, in this instance, was called a "latent" observable, not actually possessed by the electron before the measurement but yielding a definite value on measurement. Whether the electron continued on with the value exposed to the observer is a question that has been debated in the literature for decades (von Neumann's projection postulate, collapse of the wave packet). In my opinion the measurement regardless of its outcome usually and inevitably alters the state, so that a later measurement need not yield the same value as the earlier one. Numerous examples of an altered value in the second measurement can be given and the assumption implied by the customary interpretation is usually false. A single state reveals itself in numerous different effects. But this point, though closely connected with the affirmation of latency, is not of immediate interest in the present context, though it shakes the belief in the oneness of the measured value and the postmeasurement state of a physical observable.

Latent observables in quantum mechanics, in addition to those already mentioned, are spin, angular momentum, and various others ascribable to *onta* in the microcosm. But it seems that at present there are two observables which are always "possessed" in the ordinary sense. They are mass and electric charge. Of these, however, mass may lose this property because of the equivalence of mass and energy,[5] and who knows what may happen to charge!

After the publication of the paper referred to, I received encouragement in the use of the concept of latency in a personal letter from Schrödinger in which he said: "The concept has, in my opinion, a wider range of application than you propose. It might also be descriptive of such observables as number and identity of elementary entities." In other words, Schrödinger felt that a system, say an electron, might be in a state in which there would be a finite probability for its being single, or triple (one electron and two positrons), and so on; nor could the observer always be sure of the identity of certain *onta*. An extension of this reasoning was given by Heisenberg in a paper published shortly before his death in which he cautioned that certain fundamental, mechanistic, common sense concepts, such as "being composed of," "having distinct and nameable parts," may be meaningless for ultimates. His explicit reference was to quarks, which are said to be parts of other *onta*. Bohm[6] takes a similar view, concluding a recent publication as follows: "Thus one is led to a new notion of *unbroken wholeness* which denies the classical idea of analyzability of the world into separately and independently existent parts." Should this kind of denial also be necessary for consciousness, for mind, so that the question of separate minds making up or adding to the universal mind could become meaningful? Some philosophers who contributed to the Vedas and the Upanishads would clearly answer in the affirmative, and the claims of mystics to have merged with God in ecstasy provide further evidence for the numberless nature of souls.

Evidently we here approach a kind of reality that differs markedly from that conveyed by our senses. In the former the rules for establishing validity, the epistemology, take on new aspects revealing unaccustomed observables. Many of the old "common sense" landmarks and signposts disappear and can no longer be used. The old questions are no longer meaningful. Such considerations may apply to psychology and to other sciences whose domains are inaccessible to the external senses. What, for example, do we mean by the question "What is the size, shape or color of a fear or hope or of an *on*?"

A major difference between western and eastern philosophies is that the West has largely believed the rules of that section of reality accessible to the senses to be universally valid; the East on the contrary did not deem those rules to be valid at all or valid in a limited part of reality. There are, to be sure, notable exceptions. I am reminded of a statement by Evelyn Underhill, an authority on mysticism, who says that "the concept of reality, unformed and unfixed by consciousness, is completely meaningless." Elsewhere he speaks of "the game of give and take that goes on between consciousness and reality."

Spengler seems to ascribe a collective mind to civilizations, for he regards them as living beings, but as an old-style Darwinist he adds that civilizations "grow with the same sublime lack of purpose as the flowers of the field." Like most writers of his time, he ignores their beauty, their evident manifestation of purpose in our ecology and their constant form. Toynbee also viewed civilizations as organisms with a pattern of growth and decay.

Schrödinger, in his *Mind and Matter,*[7] calls on Plato, Kant, and Einstein for oblique evidence in favor of the oneness of all, matter as well as mind. Referring to Kant's view that time and space are a priori forms of intuition, while the ultimate reality, the "Ding an sich," is unknowable, he says:

The supreme importance of Kant's statement does not consist in justly distributing the roles of the mind and its object—the world—between them in the process of "mind forming an idea of the world," because, as I just pointed out, it is hardly possible to discriminate between the two. The great thing was to form the idea that this *one thing*—mind or world—may well be capable of other forms of appearance that we cannot grasp and that do not imply the notions of space and time. This means an imposing liberation from one inveterate prejudice. There probably are other orders of appearance than the space-time like.

While Schrödinger here goes beyond the point now at issue toward matters that will concern us later in this chapter, the oneness of the all implies the universality of mind if we remember that matter is a construct of the mind. As to this explicit claim that the external world—physical reality—is produced by the mind, I note here merely that this claim is in harmony with the epistemology developed previously.[8] Sensations, transcribed by rules of correspondence into coherent constructs subjected to certain metaphysical requirements, finally constitute physical reality, in essence the same for all.[9]

Schrödinger's book *Mind and Matter* contains a fascinating and provocative chapter entitled "The Arithmetical Paradox: The One-ness of Mind," i.e. of all minds. The title explains itself: in our external world we find ourselves among innumerable individuals who behave in ways which lead each of us to conclude, in accordance with the approved principles of science, that every individual has a mind similar to our own. This, he says, leads to the arithmetical paradox identifying the many with one if the individual believes in a Universal Mind. The arguments he uses in his endeavor to resolve the paradox are interesting and illuminating, and I shall present some of them here.

First, however, let us examine one feature of the common assertion that we arrive at the conclusion "Every individual has a mind similar to my own" by means of the "approved principles of science." Here one might begin to wonder. In order to establish the reality of an external object, the starting point is a protocol called sensation (P-plane). As I have pointed out repeatedly, this sensation is translated or converted into a "construct" by means of rules of correspondence (operational definitions, reification, and regulation by certain metaphysical principles). Everything in the external world, from the largest object to the smallest, owes its real character to this process. Every entity is a construct of our mind called real because it satisfies this procedure.

Does the inference that each individual has a mind conform to this view? Only in a very limited sense. The scientific process always starts with sensation that can be quantified and externalyzed. But the mind is capable of existing in innumerable states that are not sensations, and for these states psychology has not found rules of correspondence leading to numbers or other concepts accessible to detailed analysis. (Metaphors won't do, as has previously been noted.) Hence the only conclusion at present derivable from my observation that other people behave like myself is that they have similar sensations! But the mind presumably is far more complex than the sensations or the protocol experiences that assail it or are grasped by it. The conclusion affirming the existence of many minds can be reached only by an important and at present not confirmable extrapolation of the scientific method, namely, that minds, having the same sensations, must also have similar moods, feelings, memories, and conations. Otherwise I can only infer that I am surrounded by robots or automata which react to external stimuli in the same manner as I do. But let us make this extrapolation, which the scientific method tolerates but does not demand, and rejoin Schrödinger in his endeavor to solve the arithmetical paradox.[10]

He holds that there are two ways out of the number paradox: Leibnitz's doctrine of monads in prestabilized harmony and a combination of eastern philosophies as they are interpreted by western writers. Before presenting some of the details of his reasoning, I offer a brief preparatory discussion based on the nature of time and space, enlarging a view that is widely held.

The arithmetical paradox, in a sense not immediately applicable to minds, receives some support from Kant's philosophy of time and space. According to this view, time and space are modes of representation of external objects, modes generated by the mind. (They are his a priori conditions for the possibility of experience, or transcendental intuitions of the intellect.) The details of Kant's analysis have lost some of their force in the wake of more recent discoveries. Following Newton and the physics of his day, Kant proclaimed the fundamental structure of space to be necessarily Euclidean, that is, to be as simple as it could possibly be. And time was thought to "flow uniformly" under all conditions, independently of space as a separate a priori condition governing all processes in the world. Kant could not be blamed for this, for non-Euclidean geometries had not yet been formulated.

The mental, subjective character of Kant's space provides a unity and universality our sensations do not possess. We see spaces filled with objects, limited in their extents. Different spaces are differentiated by the objects they contain, within a given complex of sensations.[11] The attribution of unity, the belief that all spaces are one, arises from the fact that as we pass from one place to another we never experience an interruption in our intuition of space. We conclude that space must be one, and it must be infinite because we cannot conceive of anything related to our sensations, the primary experiences of physical reality, without it.

The same argument applies to time. We experience it directly in the flight of our consciousness, both amid external sensations and in internal awareness, both afferent and efferent, as in introspection, memory, or meditation. But like space, time appears in fragments or pieces characterized by what occurs, the momentary contents of our consciousness, and again, as in the case of space, we proclaim time to be a single and infinite duration: all times are one.

The four-dimensional space-time of Einstein and Minkowski does not alter the preceding considerations. It leaves Kant's claim of the mental origin (a cruder but simpler phrase used in place of transcendental conditions a priori) of space and time unaffected, and it creates an even larger unity by combining space and time into a single manifold. The very term *single manifold* already implies somthing like Schrödinger's arithmetical paradox. And since both time and space are of mental origin, what has here been shown may have something remotely to do with the unity of a Universal Mind. But we are far from claiming that the foregoing argument provides a proof for its existence.

Schrödinger's treatment of the paradox makes a strong appeal to eastern philosophy, which in its Atman-Brahman thesis frequently adverts to the unity of all minds and consciousnesses. To quote Schrödinger:

> This is the doctrine of the Upanishads. And not only of the Upanishads. The mystically experienced union with God regularly entails this attitude unless it is opposed by strongly existing prejudices; and this means that it is less easily accepted in the West than in the East. Let me quote as an example outside the Upanishads an Islamic Persian mystic of the thirteenth century, Aziz Nasafi.
>
> "On the death of any living creature the spirit returns to the spiritual world, the body to the bodily world. In this however only the bodies are subject to change. The spiritual world is one single spirit who stands like unto a light behind the bodily world and who, when any single creature comes into being, shines through it as through a window. According to the kind and size of the window less or more light enters the world. The light itself however remains unchanged."

He cites Aldous Huxley's "Perennial Philosophy,"[12] which

> is an anthology from the mystics of the most various periods and the most various peoples. Open it where you will and you will find many beautiful utterances of a similar kind. You are struck by the miraculous agreement between humans of different race, different religion knowing nothing about each other's existence,

separated by centuries and millennia, and by the greatest distances that there are on our globe.

Schrödinger admits that this doctrine has little appeal in the West, and he traces our tendency to belittle it to a seduction by Greek science, which is the model of our own scientific enterprise. Greek and most western science is based on objectivation and has thereby cut itself off from an adequate understanding of the mind. Schrödinger adds:

> But I do believe that this is precisely the point where our present way of thinking does need to be amended, perhaps by a bit of blood-transfusion from Eastern thought. That will not be easy, we must beware of blunders—blood-transfusion always needs great precaution to prevent clotting. We do not wish to lose the logical precision that our scientific thought has reached, and that is unparalleled anywhere at any epoch.

He holds furthermore that the identity doctrine is supported by an empirical fact: consciousness is never experienced in the plural, only in the singular. This is true even in pathological cases of a split personality, where the two persons alternate, are never present jointly, and seem to know nothing of each other. Likewise, in a dream the dreamer never identifies himself with any of the persons he dreams about, and yet they are within his consciousness.

Schrödinger then turns to another aspect of the arithmetical paradox, applying it this time to the unity of a single human mind, which should, physiologically speaking, consist of numerous sub-minds, each the mind of a single brain cell. Here he refers to important experiments by Sherrington. "One would think," Schrödinger says, "that such a 'commonwealth of cells' as each of us is would be the occasion *par excellence* to exhibit plurality if it were at all able to do so." But Sherrington's experiments[13] proved the opposite and his conclusion is worth quoting:

> Are there thus quasi-independent sub-brains based on the several modalities of sense? In the roof-brain, the old "five" senses,

instead of being merged inextricably in one another and further submerged under mechanisms of higher order, are still plain to find, each demarcated in its separate sphere. How far is the mind a collection of quasi-independent perceptual minds integrated psychically in large measure by temporal concurrence of experience? . . . When it is a question of "mind" the nervous system does not integrate itself by centralization upon a pontifical cell. Rather it elaborates a millionfold democracy whose each unit is a cell . . . the concrete life compounded of sublives reveals, although integrated, its additive nature and declares itself an affair of minute foci of life acting together . . . When, however, we turn to the mind there is nothing of all this. The single nerve-cell is never a miniature brain. The cellular constitution of the body need not be for any hint of it from "mind" . . . A single pontifical brain-cell could not assure to the mental reaction a character more unified, and non-atomic than does the roof-brain's multitudinous sheet of cells. Matter and energy seem granular in structure, and so does "life," but not so mind.

I now propose another, and a quite different, approach to a possible understanding of the unity of all minds, an approach suggested by recent developments in physics, some of which we owe to the genius of Schrödinger himself.

We treat our problem in three ways. The first is highly formal and embracive; it involves assumptions that to some readers may be questionable, but it has attractive aspects and reaches its goal.

1. Earlier in this chapter I used the theory of relativity to make a case for the union of space and time. I now extend that argument further and make it serve as evidence for a Universal Mind.

Admittedly I am about to indulge in a measure of speculation, reasoning in terms that are not demanded by present-day physical science—for this would be possible only if science were complete—but invoking ideas that it tolerates. The mind is at present beyond the kind of analysis that leads to quantification, to the use of known types of mathematics and systems of logic, and a thorough search has almost failed to convince us that this will ever be the case.

Let us begin with the concept of a world line, introduced by

Minkowski in a most successful reformulation of Einstein's theory of special relativity. I present it here in qualitative fashion, forgoing the use of mathematics.

The path of any moving particle in our familiar three-dimensional space can be represented by a "formula," actually an equation in the three coordinates x, y, and z. Knowledge of this formula identifies all the points the particle traverses but not the point it occupies at a given time. In special relativity, time enters as a fourth coordinate. When thus introduced, space becomes four-dimensional, and its character changes from Euclidean to hyperbolic.

It is perhaps noteworthy that four-dimensional space can probably not be visualized by creatures like ourselves, whose sensory equipment limits their intuition to three dimensions. Some scientists, notably Poincaré, have claimed the ability to form a sensory intuition of four-space and that one could acquire it by practice. Be that as it may, the ordinary mortal cannot. We have learned that visual comprehension is no longer necessary for a scientific understanding of the world. It may in fact be forbidden in certain domains of reality.

Any point in Minkowski's four-dimensional space is called a world point, that is, it represents an event such as the presence of a particle in three-space at a given point of time. A curve in this four-space designates a succession of events in the physical world and can therefore be taken to represent the history of an *on* as it changes or moves in time through physical three-space. Such a curve is a world line. The history of the physical universe—provided it is made up of discrete *onta*—is therefore an immense collection of world lines, represented as an enormously large set of formulas, the aggregate of which I shall call the World Formula.

Two difficulties appear at this juncture. The first arises from the circumstance that the *onta* may not be discrete, that fields, continuous space distributions of material or nonmaterial entities, are also present throughout the universe. This difficulty disappears if, as present-day nuclear physics suggests, all interactions are carried by and ultimately traceable to carriers that are *onta* in the sense in which I have used the term; among them are photons, mesons, gravitons, and perhaps tachyons and dozens more. But if continuous fields that are not reducible to *onta* are present, the World Formula can be made to include them at the expense of greater complexity.

Here quantum mechanics introduces a difficulty; for as we have seen it does not vouchsafe continuous motion in the microcosmic realm and furthermore limits the *onta*'s behavior and human knowledge to probabilities. This is an important point to which I shall return. It is not destructive to the present argument; curiously, it can later be used to enhance its appeal.

Returning then to the World Formula for discrete *onta* and fields, let us see what its knowledge would imply. Whoever possessed it and was able to interpret it in all its infinite detail could be aware of all happenings in the universe at every temporal moment. Moreover, while knowledge of the three-dimensional World Formula evaluated for a special time would allow its holder to survey all momentary happenings in space, the four-dimensional formula allows the tracing of all events in time as well.

The question of the "existence" of the World Formula is neither easy to answer nor is the answer unique. In the strict mathematical sense, its existence cannot be proved, nor could its form be determined. But the universe exists; phenomena do take place and are presumably capable of description in principle, especially if we assume that there are universal laws and even if these laws contain parameters that change in time. (There is some evidence that this may happen to the so-called constant of universal gravitation and perhaps to other forces.)

A case can thus be made for the *mathematical* existence of the World Formula; but *is it known?*

We now confront the tantalizing problem of the relation between knowledge and existence, a problem whose logical solution is by no means compulsive. It is arguable only on the basis of some metaphysical presupposition. It is clearly wrong to assert that knowledge implies or requires existence, or that existence requires (implies) knowledge. For knowledge can be erroneous, incompatible with existence. *True* knowledge of an occurrence, however, implies existence. The occurrence in this case is a segment in the process of the universe. This leaves us with the question "Does existence imply true knowledge?" I have already assumed, and given reasons for assuming, that it is knowable. But is it known?

To answer this question I rule out the possibility that the present universe has existed forever. Too many current astronomical facts speak against it. If it had a beginning, two reasonable alternatives are to be faced, aside from the absurd one holding that it sprang into being by accident. The universe must therefore have been created, together with the laws that regulate it. This leaves us with two possibilities: (1) a designer, a knower, was responsible for it genesis; he designed it like a clock, which is still running. But the clockmaker disappeared or died; (2) the clockmaker still exists and *knows* the course of the universe. I accept the second alternative.

Thus we add to the already accepted thesis—that there are no happenings which in principle can never be known—the more specific one that there are none that *are* not known. This must be regarded as a metaphysical axiom. It is tantamount to asserting that the legendary tree which fell in the forest without anybody by logical necessity being able to know it did in fact neither fall nor exist.

We are thus led to the enormous conclusion that the World Formula, being true, must be knowable, and furthermore, must be known. This conclusion makes me feel justified in introducing a Universal Mind, a mind that knows, and is perhaps a personal manifestation of, the World Formula. The common term for it is God, and we should not hesitate to use it, except for this consideration. This discourse, which led us to the Universal Mind, was entirely rational and analytic, ignoring mental states other than knowledge. God, however, is usually endowed with other qualities as well, such as compassion, concern for individual minds, justice, love, and omnipotence. These were discussed in chapter 9 but are not touched by our present reasoning.

I repeat: the foregoing arguments relating to the World Formula are not wholly rigorous in the strictest logical sense; the passage through difficult philosophic terrain via the stepping-stones of current scientific knowledge, existence of a World Formula, knowledge of the World Formula by a postulated knower, is speculative but consistent. However, it can be phrased in less mathematical form in the following way.

2. Human understanding seeks a goal; we believe it is in fact approaching it (in an asymptotic way). That goal is a valid theory accounting for everything that has happened. The words "accounts for" mean that the theory's constructs must satisfy all the rules and principles of confirmation discussed in chapter 4, and probably others as yet undiscovered. This "valid theory" is what I have called the World Formula in the present chapter.

3. My third approach is by far the simplest. It reflects the conclusions of chapter 2. There we found that the process of evolution, which in its largest sense includes all happenings, is ruled by purpose. But purpose presupposes a mind. This could only be the Universal Mind, a cosmic consciousness.

If my considerations in this chapter are correct, each individual mind is part of God or part of the Universal Mind. I use the phrase "part of" with hesitation, recalling its looseness and inapplicability even in recent physics. Perhaps a better way to put the matter is to say that each of us is the Universal Mind but inflicted with limitations that obscure all but a tiny fraction of its aspects and properties.

What, then, are the properties of the Universal Mind presented by my contention? Its knowledge comprises not only the entire present but all past events as well. Much as our throught can survey and come to know all space, the Universal Mind can travel back and forth in time at will. Its universality comprises not only the mind of each of us but is equally aware of our past. Our experience is in three-dimensional space, and time "flows" as a separate entity, only one point of which, one moment, we are able to perceive. Our time perspective is limited to one point in the four-dimensional manifold. The meaning and the effect of this curtailment is perhaps best illustrated in terms of a three-dimensional space-time metaphor.

Suppose you are traveling in the baggage car of a train with sliding doors on its sides. Open each door a trifle, so that the landscape can be seen through two opposite narrow slits. Time advances as the train moves, and the two slits allow you to see a two-dimensional world at any instant. You thus know the scenes that have passed but have no knowledge of what lies ahead.

Now proceed to the nonvisualizable case of four-dimensions. At any one time we see a three-dimensional world and we recall its past, but we know nothing of its future. We are observing one three-dimensional universe *changing* its aspects in time, as though our vision were constrained by a narrow slit in the time dimension. If the slit were opened we would see the whole world in its future as well as its past. If it is narrow we are evaluating the World Formula at a single instant; the Universal Mind, however, is aware of the entire past, and it creates the future.

This limitation of vision is one essential difference between the Universal Mind and our individual consciousness. I shall speak of this limitation as the time slit, attributing it to bodily constraints, to all the circumstances that make us seem like individuals although we are part of the Universal Mind.

Our human state inflicts further impediments on us which set us apart from the Universal Mind. One I shall call the "personal wall." It produces the prevailing sense of individual isolation and gives us an identity as well as an ego. I regard it, too, as a bodily constraint that under certain circumstances, occasioned by conditions of the body, can be more or less rigid, more or less opaque.

Added to these two impediments is a third, which is also of crucial importance in characterizing the human state. According to quantum theory there are no world lines, at least not in the microcosm. As we have seen in chapter 8, description in the microcosm is not in terms of trajectories, which are continuous chains of events. Our knowledge is limited to state functions, which imply probabilities, and the train of arguments here adopted and properly altered would lead to a World Formula that, at any time t, would spell out the probability distribution of all possible happenings. Indeed there exists still an unresolved question whether quantum mechanics could in principle lead to a World Formula including the observer himself.

There is, however, a correlated, adverse, even contradictory fact. While the future is governed by probabilities, the past is not, for what has happened can be known in detail. Here, incidentally, is another case of "reductionism" or, as I preferred to call it, "transcendence with continuity": The past is regulated by determinate and determinable causes; the future by probabilities.[14]

In a previous publication[15] I have indicated that this circumstance makes possible the freedom of our will, which would contradict science if strict determinism regarding the future prevailed. One conclusion we draw from this is that quantum mechanics, or any basic formulation of physical principles, *must* operate with probabilities, and that efforts to remove them are philosophically misguided. If there are hidden variables that remove probabilities, they are evident to the Universal Mind, not to man's knowledge. For the Universal Mind has no time slit, no personal wall; its knowledge is not limited by quantum probabilities. This means that a World Formula of the kind I have considered here is indeed descriptive of its awareness. All this is compatible with Einstein's famous utterance: *Der Herrgott würfelt nicht.*

What, then, are we to conclude? Simply that there is a third human limitation, restrictive of our knowledge but permissive of freedom. I will call it the stochastic inhibition, or stochastic wall, limiting man to probabilistic anticipation of future events.

Hence the World Formula is available to us afflicted or

modified by three human limitations: individual isolation, here called the personal wall (Schrödinger's arithmetical paradox); temporal restriction, called the time slit; and probabilistic knowledge imposed by the stochastic wall. There is a profound sense in which these are blessings within a finite human existence.

The suggestion is that in a final assessment the three restrictions are not absolute but can vary in their strictness. The last—stochastic understanding—is partially relaxed in science itself, for our description of the molar and the macroscopic world is almost free of it. What would occur if the other two were also subject to relaxation under suitable circumstances, circumstances that might have their origin in the neural system or the organization of the brain?

Speaking figuratively, a widening of the time slit would make us aware of the future; we would experience precognition. A lowering of the personal wall would enhance our sense of identity with others. This lowering of the wall might occur in cases of unusual sympathy with and love of others, in spontaneous empathy through concentrated attention, in meditations, in dreams, in personal experiences that in the terms of LeShan and others reveal alternate realities. It might occur in prayer, when an individual merges with the Universal Mind. The lowering of the personal wall might permit extrasensory perception in the form of coalescence of information, perhaps in the form of mind reading.

My theory might thus open the door to an understanding of some parapsychological effects that have attained a sufficient degree of scientific credibility to make them interesting and challenging.

At this point I take the liberty of adding a personal note. I happen to believe in the occurrence of a variety of paranormal phenomena, to which my attention was directed through participation in numerous conferences arranged by Mrs. Eileen Garrett in her beautiful summer home in Le Piol near the French Riviera. Yet I have been unable to accept explanations occasionally offered in terms of physical theories. My interest is chiefly in ESP, clairvoyance, prediction of future events, and psychokinesis. Poltergeists and visual appearance of ghosts I tend to reject. The thesis here presented—the three bodily limitations and the possibility of their relaxation—account simply for the possibility of ESP or knowledge and prediction of different events (but not for most forms of psychokinesis), and this adds in my view to the credibility of the preceding conjectures.

Certain kinds of psychokinesis that have been widely reported and verified[16] is understandable in modern physical terms. I confine my remarks here to observations in which alternative events, like the emission of particles from radioactive materials and random-generator effects, do not require different energies that need to be supplied by outside agencies. Movements of large-scale objects, the bending of keys, and similar phenomenona are therefore excluded from consideration.

The explanation of the sub-microscopic effects is similar to the resolution of the freedom-of-will problem I have discussed in previous publications.[17] The physics of the situation permits different small-scale events by virtue of quantum mechanics. The same is true about brain states. And as the mind selects from among the possible brain states when it wills an action, so could the mind of the psychokinetic agent select a permitted outcome among random events. The added hypothesis would be that the mind can influence not only my body but also another, even lifeless, object.

In this chapter I have once more approached the realm of religion, for the Universal Mind obviously presents some of the attributes of God. But to go further into theology I should have to rely more heavily on faith than I have done so far, perhaps more heavily than the scientific flavor of the book warrants. Should we believe in a dark, demonic side of the Universal Mind? I have not discussed the problem of survival of our consciousness and our memories after bodily death. What I did imply is that the conscious self will return to its presumed origin, which is the Universal Mind, and from this it seems to follow that, as part of God, it has the faculty of revisiting all aspects of its earthly experience, and perhaps even the choice of forgetting them all and consigning itself to oblivion (or even extinction). But the crucial thought, the expectation of a reunion with God, already contains some solace and hope and the promise of death as a unique experience. Even the doctrine of transmigration of souls is not at odds with my deliberations.

Here the problem of evil comes to mind again. God is continually aware of our fate and our actions, our sufferings and our happiness. To be sure he is no doubt the originator of our ethical commandments, but he seems to tolerate our transgressions. The execution of justice in this life is incomplete. But this life may not be the only one: my argument permits a great variety of conditions in afterlife (or -lives) which may compensate for what appear to be unfortunate events in the present one. Eastern religions, in the theory of Karma and the attainment of nirvana, meet this problem. The doctrine of heaven and hell does likewise, but in a crude and primitive way.

My description of what I metaphorically called the time slit is not an entirely accurate version of this bodily impediment. I have said nothing about its width, nor about the sharpness of its edges. On further consideration it will appear that its forward edge is normally sharp: we do not experience the future. The backward edge, however, is fuzzy and trails off into the past. Here memory, in part a function of our brain, links the present selectively with many occurrences of the past. In this instance the body, which I held responsible for the three previous impediments, provides an aid, a partial retention of past experiences, on which our mind can draw for information. Memory is thought to be a physiological faculty involving many neural connections and events, which are scanned by the mind. The details of the processes of importance in the laying down of memory are still an unsolved problem. Psychologists are greatly concerned with the location of specific memories within the brain. Some tend to place them in definite parts because they can be destroyed by removing or debilitating these parts. Others regard the entire brain as their focus. A physicist's reaction might be to wonder whether such conclusions are necessarily meaningful, for he has learned that there are phenomena, *onta,* or states that defy by their very nature the assignment of position or location. To be sure, specific memories seem to be encoded in the structure of the synaptic connections of the nerve cells, forming an unimaginably complex pattern. But to quote Eccles[18] again,

> . . . the read-out by the self-conscious mind involved the integration into a unified experience of the specific activities of many modules, an integration that gives the pictured uniqueness to the experience. Furthermore, it is a two-way action, the self-conscious mind modifying the modular activity as well as receiving from it and possibly evaluating it by testing procedures in an input-output manner.

The Universal Mind has no need for memory, since all things and processes—past, present, and future—are open to its grasp.

My present conjecture accounts for what is known about amnesia, the short-term loss of memory as well as retrograde and anterograde amnesia.[18] It might furthermore account for loss of memory with age.

The central thesis of this chapter is essentially a contemporary version, adjusted to recently acquired insights, of ancient views. To quote Ken Wilber,[19]

> . . . the core insight of this holistic experience is that man's innermost consciousness is identical to the absolute and ultimate reality of the universe, known variously as Brahman, Tao, Tathagata, Christ, Dharmakaya, Allah, the Godhead, or absolute Mind, to name but a few. The mystical tradition arises from this experience and asserts in one way or another that Mind is what there is and all there is, spaceless and therefore infinite, timeless and therefore eternal, outside of which nothing exists.

Elsewhere he speaks of it as *cosmic consciousness, as man's Supreme Identity.*

Of all ancient writings the Vedas and especially their successors, the Upanishads, come closest to the interpretation of existence toward which this book is heading. Far more philosophical and also more embracive than western sacred writings —and admittedly also more vague and diffusive—they contain many affirmations of the action of a Universal Mind, usually called OM or Brahman.[20]

Thus we read, for example, at the beginning of Mandukiya: "Whatsoever has existed, whatsoever exists, whatsoever shall exist hereafter, is OM. And whatsoever transcends past, present, and future, that also is OM. All that we see without is Brahman. This self that is within is Brahman."

I will also quote the preface of Chandage: "Brahman is all. From Brahman come appearances, sensations, desires, deeds. But all these are merely name and form. To know Brahman one must experience the identity between him and the self, or Brahman dwelling within the lotus of the heart."

A pupil, Gargya (in Brihadaranyaka), speaks of the sun as the supreme agency. His teacher (Ajatasatru) answers: "Nay, nay! Do not speak thus of Brahman, that being I worship is transcendental, luminous, supreme. He who meditates upon Brahman as such goes beyond all created beings and becomes the glorious ruler of all."

The pupil then praises the moon. His teacher replies, "Nay, nay! Do not speak thus of Brahman. That being I worship is infinite, clad in purity, blissful, resplendent, He who meditates upon Brahman as such lacks nothing and is forever happy." And the discourse goes on in this vein.[20]

By way of concluding this book I wish to give a summary that relates its title to its content. The word *existence* is not unique in its meaning but admits of a considerable variety of interpretations. A different one appears in each of the following sentences: The tree exists. Electrons exist. Photons exist. Life exists. Space exists. Irrational numbers exist. The limit of a mathematical series exists. Probabilities exist. I exist. You exist. My thought exists. My feeling of sadness exists. My or your hope exists. Metaphysical principles, such as the rules of correspondence and the guiding principles used in the verification of external experience, exist. The universe exists. God exists.

How are all these statements unified? The answer given in the preceding pages implies what might be called coherent degrees of existence. Ultimate existence is ascribed to the Universal Mind. In commonplace terminology we might be tempted to say that each individual mind—and I believe that creatures besides man have minds—is part of the Universal Mind. But here we encounter the arithmetical paradox and realize that the phrase "part of" again loses its meaning for ultimates, certainly in the mental realm. For even in the domain of nuclear physics we have learned that persistent identity of *onta*, constancy of their numbers, the process of a single mode of decomposition into parts, no longer explain our recently acquired knowledge. Hence the statement "we are all parts of the Universal Mind and yet we act and feel as different individuals" is by no means absurd. I regret to say that logicians have not yet caught up with this traditionally baffling situation.

I have tried to explain it by introducing three so-called bodily constraints, factors obscuring our identity with the Universal Mind because each of us has a different body, and the word "different" is here used in its conventional sense, which does apply to the molar external world. But in what sense do our bodies, which are responsible for these constraints, exist?

Here our epistemology enters the scene. All objects of the external world, including the body and all its parts, such as the brain, are constructed in absolutely and universally verifiable fashion by our minds. This is made possible because of the "existence"—the successful applicability—of universal laws of nature, for which only the Universal Mind is responsible.

I can give no cogent reason for the bodily constraints. Their possibility is in keeping with the knowledge that our body affects our mind in numerous crucial ways, even to the extent of altering our personality and our identity. Here the personal wall partly breaks down temporarily and rebuilds itself, sometimes with slightly but crucially different features.

The time slit with a certain breadth and a fuzzy back side allowing and also affecting memory may be a poor symbol of our second impediment, but I can think of none better.

The lack of solidity I imputed to these bodily constraints, their variability within certain limits, appears to be a reasonable conjecture. It accounts for differences in personality, for natural sympathy and egoism, for good and poor memory, perhaps for sleep and dreams, for an establishment of greater affinity with the Universal Mind.

Noteworthy perhaps is the promise this picture offers for an explanation of ESP (partial breakdown of two personal walls), precognition (opening of the temporally forward side of the time slit), even communication with the dead, who are presumably parts of the Universal Mind. As mentioned in chapter 8 I not only reject current physical explanations of these paranormal experiences but see no need for these explanations.

The third bodily constraint is the stochastic one: man's knowledge is always, but in varying degrees, afflicted with error and must therefore be expressed in terms of probabilities. The physicist is more acutely aware of this than other scientists when he makes a measurement. But the stochastic wall is more or less transparent, especially with respect to past events in the macrocosm and more opaque toward the future and toward microcosmic processes.

Thus, to sum up the enigma of existence, only the Universal Mind, the cosmic consciousness, possesses existence in full unlimited measure. The Universal Mind confers existence on conscious beings in varying degrees, and these beings create, out of the minds bestowed on them and in accordance with principles imposed by the Universal Mind, everything else they call real or existing.

One final word about the stochastic limitation. In the context of the speculative considerations in this book, it seems perhaps strange and less obvious than the two other "walls." The reason, I believe, is our approach from the domain of science and philosophy, which exposes only limited attributes of the Universal Mind. God's full identity, his love for human beings in their moral and even intellectual inadequacy, his apparent cruelty in the fate he often inflicts, man's attempt to understand the appearance of evil—all raise problems that science alone cannot resolve. And it is my belief that man's ignorance, and his consequent need of faith, are both lodged within the limitations of what I called the stochastic and other bodily impediments.

At this point I return briefly to the problem of evil, already discussed in the preceding chapter. The Universal Mind is supposed to possess the apparently conflicting attributes of goodness (love of human beings), omniscience, and omnipotence. The common belief is that these are contradictory: God's knowledge of the suffering he inflicts on his creatures should, because of his goodness, lead him to prevent it in view of his omnipotence. This reasoning, however, neglects two points. One is that God the creator is also responsible for the laws of nature. Many forms of evil are the results of physical, physiological, and other processes. Hence if we add the quality of consistency, action in accord with the laws he created, to the character of God, the problem of evil may disappear.

Then there is human ignorance, which may mistake ultimate good for evil. The "walls" I introduced prevent us from knowing the fate of our minds after our bodily death when there may be revealing compensation for the good and evil experienced during our human life. The effectiveness of prayer, our merging with the Universal Mind, is of course vouchsafed by the circumstance that the World Formula does not include the future. In creating it, even while obeying the laws of nature, God can doubtless be influenced by our concerns.

My account of the "walls" or limitations is doubtless incomplete. It focuses on what I would regard in retrospect as the three universal and major restrictions. There are certainly innumerable incidental ones, some of which should perhaps be mentioned. Illness is an important and complex one. In accordance with the laws of nature, which the Universal Mind created, the body's malfunctions affect the mind, causing pain, fear, and other mental accompaniments of disease. Reciprocally, it is becoming increasingly clear that mental states can in turn affect the body.

Aging is primarily the wearing out of bodily organs in conformity with the laws of nature. But it also affects the mind inasmuch as it is accompanied by a loss of memory. Speaking perhaps somewhat naively, this might simply be a solidification of what I called the time slit, an increase in sharpness of its fuzzy rear edge. However, loss of memory with age is not precisely what it is usually conceived to be, a loss of information because of the disappearance or deactivation of parts of the brain in which the item to be remembered was stored. Older people as a rule retain ideas but find themselves at a loss for their words, their names. Speech is impaired, but the thoughts as a rule are as clear as ever. Proper names tend to be forgotten but personal traits are recalled. And if the mind prompts the brain long enough, or vice versa, the name is usually recovered. Medical experts, however, often overlook these facts and regard the *mind* as deteriorating in the aging process.

Sleep is perhaps not so much a constraint as a partial removal or modification of the personal wall. It is a state in which the mind roams freely, a state in which the mind undergoes more profound changes than the body. Influencing sleep through medication has strange consequences. While the bodily accompaniments of sleep have been carefully studied (REM, the various types of brain waves), the phenomenon itself has remained a mystery. Perhaps a shift in emphasis is needed; attention should be turned to the mental aspects of sleep. Sleeping pills have no lasting benefit for the insomniac. As far as I know the best remedy is a psychic one: convince the patient that the sleep he gets is all he needs.

It is perhaps worth pointing out that my general thesis concerning the Universal Mind displays an affinity with the philosophy of Carl Jung.[21] His *synchronicity* is the simultaneous occurrence of similar phenomena at different places and in different minds, the phenomena being not causally related. A Universal Mind could bring this about. Jung's theory involves the unconscious of every individual as well as the "collective unconscious." The latter can be identified with certain aspects of the Universal Mind of which human consciousness is not aware.

Jung also introduces what he calls *archetypes*. These are mysterious agents that appear as creative or otherwise active "forces" in many human situations, although they have no temporal or spatial connection and again are not causally related. To give a significant quotation from his essay on synchronicity:

> The effective (numinous) potencies in the unconscious are the archetypes. By far the greatest number of spontaneous synchronistic phenomena that I have had occasion to observe and analyse can easily be shown to have a direct connection with an archetype. This, in itself, is an irrepresentable, psychoid factor of the collective unconscious. The latter cannot be localized, since it is either complete in principle in every individual or is found to be the same everywhere. You can never say with certainty whether what appears to be going on in the collective unconscious of a single individual is not also happening in other individuals or organisms or things or situations.

All of this can be interpreted in terms of actions of a Universal Mind.

Finally, my view has a curious and beguiling metaphysical implication: it makes the end of our deliberations flow back to their beginning. The epistemology of the first chapters is close to that of Kant. I started with sense perceptions that are converted by the intellect into constructs, which make up the things of the external world. The passage from percepts to things is controlled by what I have called metaphysical principles. In Kant's language they would be transcendental principles a priori, like space and time, and the categories. To be sure, according to more recent science these metaphysical principles are not a priori in an unalterable sense; for they may change in time as did, for instance, Kant's understanding of space.

One feature of Kant's philosophy I have made no use of, namely, his reference to things in themselves, which are the ontological originators (not to say causes) of things we conceive: our constructs. Kant regards these things in themselves as intrinsically unknowable.

My conclusion is that they might be aspects of God's thought, of the Universal Mind. We have thus arrived at the beginning of our discourse, and our imagination sees two great figures, Kant and Bishop Berkeley, shaking hands.

Postscript

After this book was written there appeared a volume so relevant to the conclusions I have reached that I could not ignore it. Its authors are the distinguished sociologist-historians O. W. Markley and Willis W. Harman.[1] *Changing Images of Man* presents and discusses the various philosophic views and social systems that have prevailed in thirteen different cultures from the Middle Paleolithic era (250,000 to 40,000 B.C.) until the present. The last dominant image is called "human as 'spirit'— the philosophia perennis [Huxley's term] view of man and the universe as essentially consciousness in manifest form." What the present book arrived at by predominantly modern scientific arguments and implied suggestions prevailed, as these authors point out, "in most cultures in various degrees of purity and at various times and places from circa 1500 B.C. to the present."

I take the liberty of repeating part of their quotation from Huxley:[2]

> *Philosophia Perennis*: the phrase was coined by Leibnitz, but the thing—the metaphysics that recognizes a divine reality substantial to the world of things and lives and minds; the psychology that finds in the soul something similar to, or even identical with, divine Reality; the ethic that places man's final end in the knowledge of the immanent and transcendent ground of all being—the thing is immemorial and universal.

What I have called the personal wall and the time slit is alluded to in the *Changing Images of Man,* whose authors say: "If the experience of individuality is but a small slit in all there is to the totality of our existence, where is the essence of the human person . . . to be found?" The Upanishads provide an answer (~ 1000 B.C.), which was implied but not boldly asserted in this book: "the atma, the Self, is never born and never dies. It is without a cause and is eternally changeless. It is beyond time, unborn, permanent and eternal. It does not die when the body dies. Concealed in the heart of all beings lies the atma, the Spirit, the Self, smaller than the smallest atom, greater than the greatest spaces." Implied here is the meaninglessness, the futility, of assigning visual attributes to nonvisual entities, one of the basic messages conveyed by quantum mechanics.

Markley and Harman search for a global image, a world view, that will be helpful in providing stability, basic understanding of goals, synthesis and happiness for the future of mankind. Typical are the following, highly significant remarks, meant to describe the consequences of the view here presented.

> Human potentiality is limitless. All knowledge, power and awareness are ultimately accessible to one's consciousness. . . .

> As a person becomes aware of the basic nature of reality [existence], he or she is motivated toward development, creativity, and movement toward the "higher Self," and becomes increasingly directed by this higher consciousness. What is called "inspiration" or "creativity" is essentially a breaking through in ordinary awareness of these higher processes.

And finally:

> Evolution occurs, physical and mental, and is directed by higher consciousness and is characterized by purpose. As humankind increases its level of consciousness, it participates more fully in this evolutionary purpose. . . . This view of man, if it can be experienced by more than the small minority of persons who have apparently realized it through the centuries would seem to provide the needed sense of direction and holistic perception and understanding which is needed.

Notes

Introduction

1. H. Margenau, *The Nature of Physical Reality* (Woodbridge, Conn.: Ox Bow Press, 1977).
2. L. LeShan and H. Margenau, *Einstein's Space and Van Gogh's Sky* (New York: Macmillan Publishing Co., 1982).

Chapter 1

1. H. Margenau, *The Nature of Physical Reality* (Woodbridge, Conn.: Ox Bow Press, 1977); also L. LeShan and H. Margenau, *Einstein's Space and Van Gogh's Sky* (New York: Macmillan Publishing Co., 1982).
2. Coulomb's law states that the force between two electric charges or magnetic poles is proportional to the product of the charges or poles divided by the square of the distance between them. Maxwell's equations are complicated relations between electric and magnetic field strengths and the charges or poles that produce them.

   If the term reduction implies merely that Coulomb's law is a special case of, or can be derived from, Maxwell's equations, it makes sense in this instance: the more complex situation includes a simpler one. This, however, is not always the case: the laws of thermodynamics do not, even in this limited sense, reduce to the laws of mechanics. Furthermore, this kind of implication is useless for the advance of science, which proceeds from the simple to the more complex. As a principle of knowledge or epistemology reductionism will be discussed in chapter 4, where it appears as a passage from a set of constructs distant from the primary (P) plane to a set closer to it.
3. To be sure certain types of precognition involving only processes in the external world, phenomena wholly independent of human hopes, desires, and volition, may be shown to contradict the second law of thermodynamics.
4. Further comments on the latency theory of observables will be found in chapter 10.
5. The x's are, of course, three-dimensional vectors.
6. See H. Margenau, *The Nature of Physical Reality* (Woodbridge, Conn.: Ox Bow Press, 1977).

7. Frederic Vester and Gerhard Henschel, *Krebs ist Anders* (Munich: Kindler Verlag, 1973).

8. A computer could, of course, be programmed to draw the conclusion that leads the mind to the additional information. I doubt, however, that it could be programmed to arrive at *all* the conclusions a mind can draw.

Chapter 2

1. G. G. Simpson, *The Meaning of Evolution* (New Haven: Yale University Press, 1949).

2. L. LeShan and H. Margenau, *Einstein's Space and Van Gogh's Sky* (New York: Macmillan, 1982).

3. H. Margenau, *The Nature of Physical Reality* (Woodbridge, Conn.: Ox Bow Press, 1977).

4. E. Laszlo, *Introduction to Systems Philosophy* (New York: Gordon & Breach, 1972).

5. C. H. Waddington, "The Theory of Evolution Today," in *Beyond Reductionism*, ed. A. Koestler and J. R. Smythies (Boston: Beacon Press, 1964).

6. E. W. Sinnott, *Matter, Mind & Man* (New York: Harper, 1957); *Cell and Psyche* (Chapel Hill: University of North Carolina Press, 1950); *The Biology of the Spirit* (New York: Viking Press, 1955); *The Problem of Organic Form* (New Haven: Yale University Press, 1963).

7. Ralph Lillie, *General Biology, a Philosophy of Organism* (Chicago: University of Chicago Press, 1945).

8. A. Koestler, *The Case of the Midwife Toad* (London: Hutchinson, 1971).

9. H. Driesch, *The Science and Philosophy of the Organism* (London: A. & C. Black, Ltd., 1908).

10. R. Lillie, *General Biology, a Philosophy of Organism* (Chicago: University of Chicago Press, 1945).

11. C. E. M. Joad, *Philosophic Aspects of Modern Science* (London: Allen & Unwin, 1943).

12. Aloys Wenzl, *Die philosophischen Grenzfragen der modernen Naturwissenschaft* (Kohlhammer, 1954).

13. M. Delbrück, "A Physicist Looks at Biology," *Academy of Arts and Sciences* 38 (1947): 73.

14. There exists at this time no completely reliable mathematical definition of randomness, which is meant by chance. Some reasons for this statement may be found in R. B. Lindsay and H. Margenau, *Foundations of Physics* (Woodbridge, Conn.: Ox Bow Press, 1981), pp. 159–67.

15. H. Shapley, ed., *Science Ponders Religion* (New York: Appleton Century Crofts, 1960).

16. J. Eccles, *The Human Mystery* (New York: Springer, 1979).

17. Eccles's account of evolution goes beyond biology and includes the

origin of the universe. This event—if it was a single event—is clearly the beginning and therefore part of the process of evolution, hence it deserves some comment here. The currently dominant view is the Big Bang theory. Eccles's account of it is based on Steven Weinberg's book, *The First Three Minutes* (London: Andre Deutsch, 1977). It is fairly well known, and we shall not repeat it here. One point, however, is of some importance in the context of our deliberations. Eccles' account starts as follows: "The cosmic fireball began about 10 to 12 billion years ago in an immense explosive outburst . . . Much can be conjectured about the first 3.5 minutes, but the origin is completely mysterious. In that time all the matter of the Universe had been created from photons . . ." Weinberg agrees with the statement concerning the mysterious origin, and he offers conjectures in keeping with current elementary-particle physics. But he, too, does not commit himself with respect to the very beginning, which is at present regarded by many as an inexplicable mystery, indeed a miracle. Furthermore, many writers regard the act of creation as a violation of the known laws of nature. Since this book will later concern itself with other phenomena related to religion and parapsychology, which are widely held to contradict basic principles of science, we venture here the assertion that many of them do not of necessity violate the most basic laws of physics. We shall at this point inquire whether in principle the creation *ex nihilo* of a highly condensed aggregate of photons can possibly be compatible with the conservation principles concerning mass and energy.

Our reasoning is similar to that employed earlier (H. Margenau, *Thomas and the Physics of 1958: A Confrontation* [Aquinas Lecture, Milwaukee: Marquette University Press, 1958]) to show that a sphere of ordinary matter satisfying a certain relation between its mass and its radius possesses no energy and no momentum and could therefore legitimately spring into being out of nothing.

This manner of creation, however, seems now unlikely because more detailed research suggests, as already mentioned, that the state preceding the Big Bang was a dense aggregation of photons. Yet similar reasoning might apply. We remember that a mass m is equivalent to an energy equal to mc^2. Photons have a mass equal to $h\nu/c^2$, where ν is the frequency, h and c have their customary meaning. We have no certain evidence that photon masses are subject to the law of gravity, but to assume it is certainly reasonable. Two gravitationally interacting photons can then have a zero energy if the ratio ν/r, ν being their frequency and r the distance between them, is about 10^{75} cgs-units. We omit the details of the very simple computation. Expressed in another way, λr, the wave length of the gamma ray (photon) times the distance between the photons, must be about 10^{-64} cm^2 (i.e., a decimal with 63 zeros preceding 1) square centimeters. The distance must therefore be extremely small and the frequency enormous. If, instead of a pair of photons, we assume an aggregate of a large number N, the factor 10^{-64} is greatly increased and becomes more reasonable.

Needless to say, I do not advance the preceding argument as a scientific theory of creation. It is meant to show that creation-out-of-nothing, though devoid of known agencies, or causes, need not contradict our present understanding of laws of physics. But we cannot account for why it happened, we can assign no cause for it. I have endeavored to show that evolution is guided by purposes as well as causes. But purposes require minds. And if a mind was involved in the process by which the universe originated, it was not man's, and we are facing a problem of religion, we are facing divine creation by a God who did not break his laws. Later parts of the book will amplify this comment.

Chapter 3

1. M. Bunge, "Emergence and the Mind," *Neuroscience* 2 (1977): 501.
2. To give an example: quantum mechanics forces us to assign reality to such elusive entities as probability fields, a purely mathematical construct that affects the behavior of atomic entities.
3. As in previous publications I use the term *on* (plural, *onta*, Greek for "being") to designate any entity whatsoever, especially when it defies ordinary intuition.
4. Cambridge University Press, 1947.
5. Wimmer Lecture, *Scientific Indeterminism and Human Freedom* (Latrobe, Penn.: Archabby Press, 1968).
6. See my Aquinas Lecture, 1958 (Marquette University Press, 1958).
7. C. G. Jung and W. Pauli, *The Interpretation of Nature and the Psyche* (New York: Pantheon Books, 1955).
8. Karl von Frisch, *The Dancing Bees* (New York and London, 1954).
9. C. U. M. Smith, *The Problem of Life* (New York: Wiley and Sons, 1976).
10. *The Human Mystery* (New York: Springer International, 1979).
11. H. H. Kornhuber, *Memory and Transfer of Information*, H. P. Zippel, ed. (New York: Plenum Press, 1973).
12. B. Libet, *Handbook of Sensory Physiology*, vol. 2, E. Iggo, ed. (New York: Springer, 19   ).
13. K. Popper and J. Eccles, *The Self and Its Brain* (New York: Springer International, 1975).

Chapter 4

1. For the sake of continuity this chapter presents in simplified form some material contained in my two previous books, *The Nature of Physical Reality* and LeShan and Margenau, *Einstein's Space and Van Gogh's Sky*. Readers familiar with this epistemology may omit or merely scan this chapter without loss of continuity of the entire treatment.

Another important treatise along similar lines is: Sigfried Müller-Markus, *Protophysics* (The Hague: Martinus Nijhoff, 1971). This book also reaches conclusions similar to those presented here, and I wish to acknowledge my indebtedness to its author for his friendship and for numerous discussions.

2. There is perhaps one (debatable) exception to this categorical statement, that is, the Weber-Fechner law.

Chapter 5

1. I use the term *sensory* to designate the "edge" of the C-field bordering the P-plane, the place of sensory constructs, objects directly perceived by our unaided senses, objectified by the simplest rule of correspondence, reification. This region of the figure includes all things that can be seen and touched. It does not contain stars and electrons, which are located in the diagram at greater distances from P in C. They belong to physical reality and may sometimes, though not always, be subjected to the rules for things.

2. K. Popper and J. Eccles, *The Self and Its Brain* (New York: Springer, 1977), p. 360.

Chapter 6

1. E. W. Sinnott, *The Problem of Organic Form* (Yale University Press, 1963).

2. See *The Nature of Physical Reality* and (with LeShan) *Einstein's Space and Van Gogh's Sky*.

3. L. LeShan, *Alternate Realities* (New York: M. Evans and Co., 1976).

4. Sharon Begley, *Newsweek*, March 1981, p. 28.

Chapter 7

1. Quoted in E. R. Taylor, *Encounter* 36 (1971): 35.

2. H. Margenau, Wimmer Lecture XX, Archabby Press, Latrobe, Penn., 1968. See also *J. Phil. Sci.* 64 (1967): 714.

3. E. H. Walker, *Psychic Exploration*, ed. E. D. Mitchell (New York: Putnam and Sons, 1974).

4. E. H. Walker and N. Herbert, in *Future Science*, ed. J. White and S. Kipner (New York: Doubleday and Co., 1977), p. 245.

5. H. Margenau, *Phys. Rev.* 49 (1936): 240; *Phil. of Sci.* 4 (1937): 337; *The Nature of Physical Reality* (Woodbridge, Conn.: Ox Bow Press, 1977) AAAS symposium, February 1978.

6. See H. Margenau, *Phys. Rev.* (1936). This paper led to a correspondence with Einstein which reinforced the arguments here presented.

7. J. Charon, *L'Esprit, cet inconnu* (Paris: A. Michel, 1977).

8. V. A. Firsoff, *Life, Mind and Galaxies* (Edinburgh and London: Oliver and Boyd, 1967).

9. A. Koestler. Random House, 1972.
10. *Handbook of Parapsychology,* ed. B. B. Wolman (Litton Educational Publishing Co., 1977).
11. J. White and S. Kipner, eds., *Future Science* (New York: Doubleday and Co., 1977).
12. *Future Science,* p. 115.
13. *Future Science,* p. 176.
14. *Future Science,* p. 184.
15. *Future Science,* p. 245.
16. *Future Science,* p. 281.

Chapter 8

1. The symbol ψ is commonly used by physicists to designate the state function of Schrödinger. In essence, it denotes a probability field. The same symbol is employed by parapsychologists in reference to a (psychological) field that they endeavor to study. Since we may later be forced to consider parapsychology, we henceforth use the symbol φ for the *phy*sicists' state function and ψ for the *psy*chologist's "psychic" field, whatever that may be.
2. *Einstein's Space and Van Gogh's Sky* (New York: Macmillan, 1982).
3. This fact is beginning to be recognized in brain research. The search for definite locations in the brain at which mental states and physiological movements are activated, which showed some success, especially when it correlated the paralysis caused by a stroke with damage in the opposite brain hemisphere, has been drawn into question. In *Science Digest* (March 1981) we read, evidently in confirmation of Przibram's holistic theory of memory (which also seems to lack definite location): "When a monkey is taught to open and close a latched box and then has extensive portions of its brain removed, its actions are slow, but it can still open and close the box. This learned ability appears to be holistically dispersed throughout the monkey's brain rather than confined to a specific center."

Chapter 9

1. H. Margenau, *Religious Doctrine and Natural Science, Physics, and Philosophy, Selected Essays* (Holland: D. Reidel Publishing Co., 1978).
2. W. G. Pollard, *Chance and Providence* (New York: Charles Scribner's Sons, 1958).
3. H. Margenau, *Philosophy of Science* 19 (1952): 193.
4. C. von Weizsäcker, *The History of Nature* (Chicago: University of Chicago Press, 1949).
5. "The Judgement Seat," S. Maugham, *The Complete Stories of S. Maugham* (New York: Doubleday and Co., 1953), p. 500.
6. In this context, see note 1, p. 337.

7. This point has been made at length in *Einstein's Space and Van Gogh's Sky* (New York: Macmillan, 1982) and in LeShan, *Alternate Realities* (New York: M. Evans and Co., 1976).
8. H. Margenau, *Ethics and Science* (Huntington, N.Y.: R. E. Krieger Publishing Co., 1979).
9. *Ethics and Science.*

Chapter 10

1. For further information see, for example, Archie Bahm, *The World's Living Religions* (New York: Dell Publishing Co., 1964).
2. L. LeShan and H. Margenau, *Einstein's Space and Van Gogh's Sky* (New York: Macmillan, 1982).
3. H. Margenau, *Phil. of Sci.* 16 (1940): 287.
4. As a rule, not the one previously possessed because of the disturbance by the measuring apparatus.
5. *Onta* of greater mass may be formed as higher energy states of another *on*!
6. D. Bohm and B. Hiley, *Foundations of Physics,* vol. 5, 1975, p. 93.
7. E. Schrödinger, *Mind and Matter* (Cambridge: Cambridge University Press, 1959).
8. See chapters 3–6 of note 2 or the *Nature of Physical Reality.*
9. Schrödinger continues in this vein, adds the Boltzmann-Gibbs theory of entropy increase to the contributions of Kant and Einstein, and ends the chapter by claiming that "physical theory in its present stage strongly suggests the indestructibility of mind by time" (*Mind and Matter*).
10. In his book *What Is Life?* (Cambridge University Press, 1944) he proposes, not perhaps as a solution of the paradox but as a memorable metaphor, the reflection of a single object in a multitude of mirrors.
11. There exists an even greater variety of spaces if one includes alternate realities in his considerations. See note 2 above.
12. Aldous Huxley, *Perennial Philosophy.* See note 7.
13. See Sir Charles Sherrington, *Man and His Nature,* Gifford Lectures, 1937–38 (Macmillan Co., 1941).
14. The "fact" that "exact" predictions can be made in some areas of "classical" physics does not contradict this statement, the allusion to the universality of the stochastic wall. For the "fact" is wrong. Even the most precise observation leading to a prediction is subject to a finite error, however small, and this makes the prediction probabilistic to some, perhaps very slight, degree, but in principle. Cf. chap. 8.
15. Note 2. A more extended discussion may be found in H. Margenau, *Scientific Indeterminism and Human Freedom,* Wimmer Lecture XX (Latrobe, Penn.: Archabby Press, 1968).
16. In this connection I should like to mention especially the work of A. Schmidt and C. Honorton.
17. See note 15.

18. See J. C. Eccles, *The Human Mystery* (New York: Springer International, 1979), pp. 187–93.

19. Ken Wilber, "Psychologia Perennis," *Journal of Transpersonal Psychology* 2 (1975).

20. The following quotations are from the superb translation of twelve important Upanishads by Swami Prabhavananda and F. Manchester. The Vedast Society of Southern California, 1948.

21. See, for instance, C. G. Jung, "Synchronicity, on a Causal Principle" in *The Interpretation of Nature and the Psyche* (New York: Bollingen Foundation, Inc., 1955).

Postscript

1. O. W. Markley and Willis W. Harman, *Changing Images of Man* (New York: Pergamon Press, 1982).

2. A. Huxley, *The Perennial Philosophy* (New York: Harper and Bros., 1945).

Also in New Science Library:

Quantum Questions: Mystical Writings of the World's Great Physicists, edited by Ken Wilber

The Second Medical Revolution: From Biomedicine to Infomedicine, by Laurence Foss and Kenneth Rothenberg

A Sociable God: Toward a New Understanding of Religion, by Ken Wilber

Space, Time and Medicine, by Larry Dossey, M.D.

The Sphinx and the Rainbow: Brain, Mind and Future Vision, by David Loye

Staying Alive: The Psychology of Human Survival, by Roger Walsh, M.D.

The Tao of Physics: An Exploration of the Parallels between Modern Physics and Eastern Mysticism, second edition, revised and updated, by Fritjof Capra

Transformations of Consciousness: Conventional and Contemplative Perspectives on Development, by Ken Wilber, Jack Engler, and Daniel P. Brown

The Tree of Knowledge: The Biological Roots of Human Understanding, by Humberto Maturana and Francisco Varela

Up from Eden: A Transpersonal View of Human Evolution, by Ken Wilber

Waking Up: Overcoming the Obstacles to Human Potential, by Charles T. Tart

The Wonder of Being Human: Our Brain and Our Mind, by Sir John Eccles and Daniel N. Robinson